MW00584188

Mental Models:

30 Thinking Tools that Separate the Average From the Exceptional. Improved Decision-Making, Logical Analysis, and Problem-Solving.

By Peter Hollins,
Author and Researcher at
petehollins.com

Table of Contents

8

Chapter 1. Decision-Making for Speed and Context

The name Charlie Munger might not ring a bell, but you're probably familiar with his business partner, Omaha billionaire Warren Buffett, one of the world's most famous investors and, accordingly, one of the world's richest people for decades running.

The two of them have worked side by side for Buffett's multi-conglomerate Berkshire Hathaway since 1978. Although Munger isn't in the spotlight as much as his partner, Buffett credits an overwhelming amount of his success to his alliance with him. And in recent years, Munger has begun to build a following in his own right based on how he has articulated his approach to life.

This mostly began when Munger emerged from the shadows to give a commencement speech at USC Business School in 1994 entitled "Lesson on Elementary, Worldly Wisdom as It Relates to Investment Management & Business." The impact of Munger's speech has proven to be highly influential in the decades after it was delivered, as it introduced the concept of "mental models," which was subsequently disseminated to the public at large. He mused,

> What is elementary, worldly wisdom? Well, the first rule is that you can't really know anything if you just remember isolated facts and try and bang 'em back. If the facts don't hang together on a latticework of theory, you don't have them in a usable form. You've got to have models in your head. And you've got to array your experience—both vicarious and direct—on this latticework of models.

You may have noticed students who just try to remember and pound back what is remembered. Well, they fail in school and in life. You've got to hang experience on a latticework of models in your head.

What are the models? Well, the first rule is that you've got to have multiple models—because if you just have one or two that you're using, the nature of human psychology is such that you'll torture reality so that it fits your models, or at least, you'll think it does. You become the equivalent of a chiropractor who, of course, is the great boob in medicine.

It's like the old saying, "To the man with only a hammer, every problem looks like a nail." And of course, that's the way the chiropractor goes about practicing medicine. But that's a perfectly disastrous way to think and a perfectly disastrous way to operate in the world.

So you've got to have multiple models. And the models have to come from multiple disciplines—because all the wisdom of the world is not to be found in one little academic department. That's why poetry professors, by and large, are so unwise in a worldly sense. They don't have enough models in their heads. So you've got to have models across a fair array of disciplines.

You may say, "My God, this is already getting way too tough." But, fortunately, it isn't that tough—because eighty or ninety important models will carry about ninety percent of the freight in making you a worldly wise person. And of those, only a mere handful really carry very heavy freight.

He went on to emphasize at a later point,

> You must know the big ideas in the big disciplines and use them routinely—all of them, not just a few. Most people are trained in one model—economics, for example—and try to solve all problems in one way. You know the old saying: to the man with a hammer, the world looks like a nail. This is a dumb way of handling problems.

While I wouldn't go so far as to say that having deep expertise in a discipline is *dumb*, it's certainly not an optimal or efficient way of solving or understanding situations that life will toss your way. It leaves you woefully unequipped for whatever lies outside your primary knowledge base, but the answer isn't to become an expert in every field. It's finding your own *latticework of mental models*.

Thus, Munger makes it clear that to navigate the world without a set of mental models is tantamount to blindfolding yourself and randomly pointing to a spinning globe while trying to find Cuba. Without mental models as a blueprint to guide your thinking, you are only able to see haphazard, individual elements with no connection to each other.

To continue with his hammer analogy, if you are working on a construction site, it would serve you well to know how to use a hammer, saw, nails, drill, sander, and so on. The more tools you are familiar with, the better you can handle different and novel construction jobs; the more mental models you acquire, the better you can deal with and understand old and new life occurrences.

So what exactly is a mental model?

It's a blueprint to draw your attention to the important elements of whatever you are facing, and it defines context, background, and direction. You gain understanding even if you lack actual knowledge or experience, and the ability to make optimal decisions.

For instance, if you are an aspiring chef, most of what you end up learning amounts to mental models: what kind of flavor profiles exist, what basic ingredients are needed for a stock or a sauce, typical techniques to use for different meats, and the conventional beverage and food pairings. Understand those, and you will generally know how to handle yourself with any type of cuisine. Absent a latticework of underlying models, each new recipe would present entirely new struggles.

Although many are universal, different situations will require different types of blueprints—and that's why Munger so emphasized the latticework of mental models so as to be prepared in as many situations as possible. Without a mental model, you might see only a random assortment of lines. But *with* an applicable mental model, it's like being handed a map to what all those lines mean—now you can correctly interpret information and make an informed decision.

Mental models provide an understanding of the situation, and predictable results for what will happen in the future. You can call them life heuristics or guidelines to evaluate and comprehend. You can also think of them as a set of goggles you can strap on when you want to focus on a specific goal.

You might be thinking that no model is an entirely perfect reflection of the world, but they don't have to be. They just need to point us in the right direction to the complexity around us and filter the signal from the noise. Anyway, that's better than the alternative of being completely blind.

We each already have our own mental models gleaned from years of simply living and noticing patterns of everyday life. Most of us have an idea of how to act in a fancy restaurant because we've been exposed to it in some way. We also have a set of mental models based on our values, experiences, and unique worldviews. You may refuse to use banks out of distrust for large institutions and keep your money tucked under your mattress as a rule of thumb—no one ever said all mental models are useful, accurate, or widely applicable. Indeed, some can consistently lead us down the wrong path.

By definition, our personal mental models are limited and only reflect a biased perspective.

If *my* mental approach is the *only* thing I use when I'm trying to perceive and understand the world, I'm not going to have a very broad spectrum of comprehension about the world. Invariably, I will get some things completely wrong and would come up blank in other situations when nothing in my experience can apply.

That's where this book comes in. I want to introduce a latticework of mental models for you to operate better in the world. Some are specific, while some are universal and widely applicable. They will all assist you in thinking more clearly, making better decisions, and finding clarity in confusion.

Seeing the same object or event through different mental models will give you vastly different perspectives based on what you are focusing on, and certainly a wider array than if you would have just stuck to your own frame of reference. The more varied perspectives you possess, the more of the world we can understand.

Our aspiring chef from earlier can view a basket of ingredients through a baker's lens, a classic French chef's lens, a sandwich artist's lens, or a Szechuan Chinese chef's lens. None of these models is necessarily the most optimal, but they give you a frame of reference as opposed to just staring at a bunch of ingredients and not having any idea of what to do with them.

Perhaps the most important part of mental models is that they act to prevent human error—appropriately, another one of Munger's famous speeches was titled, "The Psychology of Human Misjudgment."

With too few mental models, you risk falling prey to the fable of the blind men and the elephant, which goes something like the following; there were once six blind men, and they all reached out and could only feel different parts of an elephant: the knee, the side, the tusk, the trunk, the ear, and the tail. None of these blind men were wrong in isolation, but they could only see from a single perspective, so they were wrong about the elephant's overall appearance.

Multiple models challenge each other to produce a more unified overview, whereas just using one or two restricts your long-range view to a limited context or discipline. Having a huge range of mental models can expand your viewpoint and cancel out some of the stray "errors" that using just one or two models would produce.

This doesn't mean you have to know all the ins and outs of a million different disciplines to use multiple mental models. You just need to understand the basic points and fundamentals of a few essential ones. Just don't be the person with a single hammer.

This first chapter delves deeply into decision-making mental models. In a sense, most mental models eventually help us with decisions, but these specific models are about how to process information more quickly and find an outcome that you are more likely to be happy with. In other words, they get you from Point A to Point B in less time, and they might also help you define what Point A actually is.

Most of the time with decisions, we are overloaded with information—the classic signal-to-noise ratio problem. You will learn to become selectively deaf and only intake what matters. That's where we start with the first mental model.

MM #1: Address "Important"; Ignore "Urgent"

Use to separate true priorities from imposters.

Even when we are relaxing, we can fall into sudden panic and feel a rush of adrenaline when we try to make a decision. We can be as cool as a cucumber, lounging in a pool, and still have this feeling. Why is that?

This is our brain fooling us into one of the most dangerous fallacies—one that will keep you perpetually focusing on what doesn't matter. Everything, seemingly, is an emergency to be handled as soon as humanly possible, and horrible consequences will follow if you don't personally act.

The mistake is thinking of "important" and "urgent" as synonymous and not realizing the huge gulf of difference between the two terms and how you should prioritize them. The ability to distinguish the two is a key step in lowering your anxiety, stopping procrastination, and making sure that you are acting in an optimized way.

This mental model probably has the most cache in the realm of productivity, where time is at a premium. We spend far too much time on *urgent* tasks when we should be focusing on *important* tasks.

Important task: These contribute directly to our short-term or long-term goals. They are absolutely imperative to our work, responsibilities, or lives. They cannot be skipped and should be prioritized. They may not need to be done immediately and thus don't appear to be important. This makes it easy to fall into the trap of ignoring the important for the urgent. But they are what truly impact your various bottom lines, and serious negative repercussions would follow from skipping them.

Urgent task: These simply demand immediacy and speed, and usually come from other people. Of course, this naturally creates a reaction on your end that can make us forget what's important. They *can* overlap with an important task, but they can also just demand your immediate attention without deserving it. These are usually smaller and easier to complete, so often we turn to them out of procrastination, and it allows us to feel quasi-productive even though we've ignored what we *really* need to be doing. Many urgent tasks can be delayed, delegated, or flat-out ignored.

As a quick example, if you are an author under a tight deadline, an *important* task for you would be to continue writing your book. You need to hit 5,000 words a day for the next two weeks or else you are going to be eating bread and oatmeal. This would qualify as a priority.

An *urgent* task would be dealing with that annoying "check engine" light that keeps flickering on and off in your car. Your car can probably survive a few more trips, and even though the light winking can be seductive, you need to resist it, because this is urgent masquerading as important.

Typically, you'll find that an important activity or project might not have that many urgent tasks connected with it. This tends to cause confusion of priorities. Luckily, there is a tried and true method of distinguishing between urgent and important, and the method draws its name from one of the most famous American presidents, Dwight D. Eisenhower. It's called the Eisenhower Matrix, and it will help you prioritize and identify what you really need to be juggling at the moment.

Eisenhower was a five-star general during World War II before being elected president and serving two presidential terms from 1953 to 1961. In addition to leading the

Allied forces to victory in the war, Eisenhower oversaw the creation of NASA, the American interstate highway system, and new civil rights legislation while navigating the United States through the Korean conflict and the instigation of the Cold War.

To master his impossibly complicated schedule, Eisenhower developed a system that helped him sort his activities and demands into matters that were most important and identify the most vital processes to serve those important elements. It also helped him determine which less-essential tasks he could either designate someone else to complete or eliminate entirely. In other words, important versus urgent.

Some tasks could lead to new civil rights legislation but never quite appear urgent. Other tasks could appear to be screamingly urgent but would never make a difference either way. Any person, especially one as impactful as the President of the United States, should simply know what matters.

Eisenhower's matrix is easy for anyone to employ and goes a long way toward improving efficiency and accomplishment. The template is a simple two-by-two grid divided between "important" goals and "urgent" tasks, as seen below.

The Eisenhower Matrix

	Urgent	Not Urgent
Important	DO it today	SCHEDULE a time to do it
Not Important	DELEGATE it to someone else	ELIMINATE Stop doing this

www.expertprogrammanagement.com

Important tasks. The top row of the matrix represents the most important obligations or responsibilities one has in their life. These are things that require our most mindful and active attention. For work, these might include the most pertinent aspects of our job descriptions—overseeing a budget, managing a long-term project that defines our business, or maintaining constant operations. For personal matters, it could mean directing our health (or that of our loved ones), sustaining a relationship or marriage, selling a house, or establishing a business. Whatever things most impact every other thing in our lives or work are the most important.

However, just because something is extremely important doesn't mean every activity that supports it needs to be done immediately. Some can be put on the backburner (indefinitely, even), some aren't even ready to be dealt with, and some depend on other people moving first. In short, you can't do them all *right now*. That's where the "urgency" metric comes in: the top row of the matrix is thus divided according to what can happen now and what can be delayed (but must happen at some point in the future).

Urgent: Do. Objects in the "do" quadrant are things that absolutely need to be done posthaste. They must be completed to stave off unfavorable outcomes or uncontrollable circumstances, and the sooner they're done, the less work (and more relief) there will be in the future. "Do" tasks typically revolve around deadlines: final term papers, court filings, car registrations, school applications, and so forth.

They also include emergencies or activities that need to be completed to avert disaster. "Do" tasks are best thought of as duties that need to be completed immediately, by the end of today, or tomorrow at the very latest. They cause anxiety because they're high-effort duties that you dread doing but need to do nevertheless.

Not urgent: Plan. Tasks that reside in the second quadrant need to be done at some point—but not necessarily *now*. The world isn't going to collapse if they're not done today; they're not on a strict deadline to be completed. Still, they have to be done at *some* point, usually relatively soon, so they need to be scheduled. "Plan" tasks include setting up a future meeting with a big client, arranging a time for a roof leak to be fixed, studying or reading class materials or work documents, or maintenance duties that cover the long term.

Schedule them after the fires are put out. Plan them for the near future, but not so imminent that it interferes with your truly urgent *and* important tasks. "Plan" tasks are also key components of your medium-to-long range plans: when you're planning a week or a month or advance, "plan" tasks should be put on your timetable.

The danger with these "not urgent" tasks is deprioritizing them too much. They're important to keep normal operations afloat, and if they're discarded or forgotten, they may well turn into emergency tasks in short order. Take the "check engine" light in your car from earlier—anecdotally, I have driven with that light on for close to a year and nothing terrible has happened, so even though it's theoretically important, it doesn't demand urgent attention.

Not-important tasks. The bottom row of Eisenhower's matrix represents tasks that aren't that significant to you personally. That doesn't mean they're unimportant to other people (though it might), but they're activities that might be more appropriate or meaningful for somebody else to finish up.

Other people will certainly attempt to present them as important to you, but they're often just projecting their own self-interests. Is there an impact on you? Minimal, if any. The not-important tier is also divided up by relative urgency.

Urgent: Delegate. Perhaps the most befuddling square in this matrix is the "not-important but urgent" box. It perhaps makes the most sense in a work environment: these are tasks that might really need to be done, but it's not vital for *you* to take care of them yourself, even if you could. If you *did* complete them yourself, they might impose on the "important" items that you absolutely have to do either now or later.

For those reasons, items in this box should be eliminated, preferably by being delegated to somebody else. When you're working as the leader of a team, you should be able to find someone else to handle these tasks for you.

Not-important/urgent tasks can be identified by measuring how vital they are to what's happening now. These can very generally be described as interruptions: phone calls, emails, ongoing family situations, and so forth. During times of inactivity these all may be important to focus on, but at the moment they could distract or misdirect you from what you have to get accomplished toward your overall goals.

You may be fielding customer support emails even though you are the CEO of the 100-person company. These customer support emails represent extremely angry and disturbed clients, and they're urgent to everyone involved—except you.

There really is no point or importance for you to be involved in this daily minutia, and thus, you must eliminate it from your schedule through delegation.

Not urgent: Eliminate. Finally, there are some activities and functions that are neither important nor time-sensitive to the priorities at hand. What are they even there for? Mostly to distract you or serve as an escape from doing what you need to do:

leisure activity, social media, binge-watching, long phone calls, extensive hobby time, and so forth. In the name of efficiency and prioritizing, these things are dead weight—we might not always be optimizing for those things, but it is still helpful to simply know.

These are just things that grab your attention for one reason or another and try to force a response; they're even hard to name sometimes because they feel so insignificant and fleeting. But they add up. (If you ever want to shock yourself and see how much they add up, install trackers on your phone and computer to see how much time you log on truly useless pursuits.)

These are the activities you shouldn't account for in your schedule at all and should only be done when everything else is completed. Only keep items that are important to the bottom-line success of your project or life. This doesn't mean you can't *ever* do them (and you'd be mistaken not to allow yourself a little bit of escapism now and then). But when you're in the middle of other important items that need your attention or oversight, take them off your plate completely. They'll be more meaningful and rewarding when you've finished the important tasks anyway.

Just because something appears to demand a quick response doesn't mean you should give it, and just because something is slowly ticking in the background doesn't mean you should ignore it. Learn to balance the two for optimal decisions.

MM #2: Visualize All the Dominoes

Use to make decisions that are as informed as possible.

When faced with the need to make a decision, most of us only consider the immediate impact that decision will have—especially if it's a time-sensitive or urgent one. We think in terms of one domino ahead; life is never so simple and quarantined. What about the rest of the dominoes? They don't simply disappear.

We perceive most of our everyday decisions as isolated situations that don't have a ton of consequences, positive or negative. We practice a disturbing lack of foresight on a daily basis because that's how we're biologically wired as humans, and yet our instincts don't serve us very well here. Typical human thinking cannot be faulted: I step on a nail, and I jump to the side in pain and end up falling off a cliff. It just happens.

This is generally known as first-order thinking, and it is where we focus exclusively on resolving a question or decision at hand and don't consider the more long-lasting ramifications or how our decision will play out in the distant future. If it helps, call it *first-domino thinking*.

But many of our decisions, especially the ones we toss and turn over at night, have consequences that extend beyond what we can see right before us. In terms of consequences, humans are as blind as bats. Small decisions one might make could result in effects down the road they didn't foresee, resulting in a sort of butterfly effect. The outcome isn't just limited to the immediate changes we've decided upon—other people or situations can be affected as well. Some of them may have been truly unpredictable, and some might be invisible until they rear their ugly heads. Others, though, only catch us by surprise because we didn't think the situation through quite deeply enough.

Okay, you've heard enough about what *not* to do, so what *should* we do? Visualize all the dominoes, otherwise known as *second-order thinking*.

This is simply trying to project into the future and extrapolate a range of consequences that you can use to conduct a cost-benefit analysis for your decisions or solutions. Instead of merely being satisfied about buying a new apartment, think about what it means for your credit, debt, and ability to own a huge dog in the future. Instead of bleaching your hair every week, consider that your bald spots have been increasing due to the harsh bleach and that a toupee may be soon necessary.

Yes, second-order thinking has the usual effect of making you think twice about what you're doing and helps eliminate rash decisions, as you might expect when you consider the prolonged aftermath of your choices. It's the practice of seeking out as much information as possible to make measured decisions.

What's the first domino to fall after a decision? Now what are the three paths that can lead to? And where do those lead? You simply don't stop your analysis once the most obvious situations are articulated. Instead, you consider as many long-term, possible ramifications as you can. How will your decision cause other dominoes to fall? If you tip this domino, which other dominoes will you be unable to tip because of time or effort (opportunity cost)?

Famous investor Howard Marks provides a dead simple way this can apply to daily life:

> A good example can be seen in the hypothetical newspaper contest John Maynard Keynes wrote about in 1936. Readers would be shown 100 photos and asked to choose the six prettiest girls, with prizes

going to the readers who chose the girls readers voted for most often. Naive entrants would try to win by picking the prettiest girls. **But note that the contest would reward the readers who chose not the prettiest girls, but the most popular.** Thus the road to winning would lie not in figuring out which were the prettiest, but in predicting which girls the average entrant would consider prettiest. Clearly, to do so, the winner would have to be a second-level thinker. (The first-level thinker wouldn't even recognize the difference.)

This can be carried one step further to take into account the fact that other entrants would each have their own opinion of what public perceptions are. Thus the strategy can be extended to the next order and the next and so on, at each level attempting to predict the eventual outcome of the process based on the reasoning of other agents.

"It is not a case of choosing those faces that, to the best of one's judgment, are really the prettiest, nor even those that average opinion genuinely thinks the prettiest. We have reached the third degree where we devote our intelligences to anticipating what average opinion expects the average opinion to be. And there are some, I believe, who practice the fourth, fifth and higher degrees." (Keynes, *The General Theory of Employment, Interest and Money*, 1936).

Think about it this way: very rarely does something happen with no chain of events to follow. It's your job to look past the positive reinforcement and gratification you may receive, which frankly may be blinding you, and understand what could go wrong, how wrong it could go, and why it might go wrong. What if you viewed each decision as having the potential to topple 15 other dominoes and set about identifying them? *Tedious yet informative.*

Second-order thinking allows you to project the totality of your decisions. Even if you don't change your decision because of what you determine through second-order thinking, you think through ten times as many scenarios and thus make far more informed choices than you would otherwise. Sometimes, that's the best we can do as a person. We can't predict the future, but we can't not think about it.

If second-order thinking's so great, then why doesn't everybody do it? Because it's hard. Humans aren't a shining example of doing the right thing on a consistent basis. Just look at our diets and how much money the weight loss industry generates on an annual basis. Questioning how our actions will affect situations beyond what's right in front of us takes probing into the unknown and leads one into a labyrinth of thinking that can be strenuous or complicated. Other people might say we're "overthinking" a decision or problem.

The fact is, second-order thinking allows you to think clearly—at least more clearly than your competition. Most of the time, that matters. Nobody ever rises above average through making the obvious choices or accepting the most convenient, simplest answers. Being able to project and foresee happenings on a deeper, futuristic level is a hallmark of successful people and almost always turns out to be worth the extra effort. Adopting this mental model will improve your decision-making and stop letting things slip through the cracks.

To think in a second-order fashion, Howard Marks provides some guiding questions.

How broadly will this decision affect things in the future? What will your decision do beyond change your immediate concerns? What concerns will be *created*? Will your decision's purpose be fulfilled?

Which result do I think will happen? Think beyond the simple resolution of the most immediate problem: if you take this course of action, what effect will it have if it succeeds or fails? What do those outcomes look like? What do semi-success and semi-failure look like? This naturally leads to the next question.

What are the chances that I will succeed or be right? From an objective standpoint as possible, what is the probability that your assessment is accurate? Is your prediction realistic or at least a little steeped in fantasy or paranoia? Every decision has a cost-benefit ratio to it. Are you too openly courting failure or semi-failure?

What does everybody else think? Hopefully you have access to at least one or two people—optimally more—who will give you an honest opinion about your prediction and whether they think you're on the right track or not. Although you shouldn't be unduly swayed by popular opinion, it's beneficial to know how your forecast is received. Consensus in numbers isn't really something to be preached, but rather, a complete lack of reality usually works alone, so you are really just trying to prevent the latter.

How is what I think different from everyone else? What are the prime splitting points between what you think and what popular knowledge and opinion dictates? What specific aspects of your information and prediction are different and why? What are they based on? What could I be missing? And again, this naturally leads to the final point.

What dominoes do other people visualizing falling? Regardless of whether you actually have someone to bounce your ideas off of, the point of this last question is to step out of your own biased perspective and view decisions as other people. Actively seek out and articulate the domino chain that other people might see, and see how the dominoes fall from their perspective. Not all perspectives are valid, but this gives you more information.

Remember, this mental model's purpose is to expose and inform. We can't circumvent our human instinct of jumping to conclusions and deciding on a whim entirely, but we can be a bit more methodical about decision factors.

This mental model very well could have been named "Ignore the Monkey's Paw" but that seemed unnecessarily morbid. So instead, I'll just briefly recount the origins of the Monkey's Paw and you can decide for yourself which is more effective in forcing you to examine secondary consequences.

The Monkey's Paw is a short story written by W.W. Jacobs in 1902. It's about a man who finds a blessed (or cursed?) monkey's paw, which will grant him three wishes. Little does the man know that even though each wish will be *technically* fulfilled, there will be harsh consequences.

For his first wish, he wishes for $200. The next day, his son is killed at work, and the company gives the man $200 as payment.

For his second wish, he wishes for his son back. In a short amount of time, he hears a knock at the door, and when he peers outside, he discovers that it is his son's mutilated and decomposing body. Frightened beyond belief, his third wish is for his son to disappear. Unintended consequences matter!

MM #3: Make Reversible Decisions

Use to strategically remove indecision whenever you can and have an action bias.

In theory, decision-making is easy. Some people do it with their gut, some try to do it with their brain, and some do it entirely out of self-interest—*what's in it for me?*

That said, decision-making is not our goal—*optimal* decision-making combined with speed is. To improve the second portion—speed—we must understand the mental model of distinguishing between reversible and irreversible decisions and how it helps us take action more quickly.

One of the biggest reasons we have for inaction is the anxiety associated with the seeming finality of decisions. We are conditioned to think that there is no turning back, and to be a "man/woman of our word."

To be blunt, this approach is dead wrong and will keep you standing on the sidelines for longer than needed. Not all decisions have to be set in stone. Most are actually written in pencil. Most are completely changeable, and approaching decisions as such will lead you to action more often than not. For instance, do you feel more comfortable buying a car on "final sale" (irreversible) or if there is a 100% money-back guarantee (reversible)? What about with painting a bathroom (reversible) versus adding a new bathroom (irreversible)? What about shaving your cat (irreversible) versus dying its hair (reversible)? The circumstances where you would feel more comfortable taking immediate action are all more reversible in nature.

Being able to tell the difference between reversible/irreversible decisions is one of the keys to speed. Add this to your decision-making analysis: *how can I make this decision reversible, and what would it take? Can I do it?* Then do that.

But knowing the difference also gives you a whole lot of information that would be impossible to know otherwise.

That's because action will almost always tell you more than analysis before the fact. When you buy a car, you are likely buying it without knowing how it will truly perform on a day-to-day basis. If you had a 100% money-back guarantee, you would buy the car instantly and gain valuable information about how it performs every day for you. Then, depending on your level of satisfaction, you can reverse the decision or not; either way, you will be extremely informed and confident in your decision. Not distinguishing between reversible/irreversible makes you slower and more ignorant.

Reversing a decision is rarely going back on your word; it's just adjusting your position in the face of new information. You'd be silly not to. Thus, *make more reversible decisions.* It doesn't matter if you're right or wrong, but you lose nothing, you gain information, and if you end up deciding correctly/optimally, you're ahead of the pack. The worst-case scenario is you're right back where you started, which isn't so bad.

Those that are still wringing their hands about a reversible decision are just losing precious time, falling behind, and using incomplete information. Architect Wernher Von Braun had this to say on the matter: "One good test is worth a thousand expert opinions."

Knowing the difference between reversible and irreversible decisions can dictate the pace and momentum of your life. If you favor reversible decisions, you keep yourself always in motion and learning. You're not overanalyzing or becoming mired in analysis paralysis. You're not the proverbial *Buridan's donkey*, the morose donkey who was stuck between two bales of hay and starved to death as a result of indecision and analysis. This may not change your thought process of irreversible decisions, but those shouldn't be rushed, anyway. For everything else, you have nothing to lose and can only gain.

Jeff Bezos, the founder of Amazon.com, who bears an increasing resemblance to Lex Luthor and is, as of this writing, the richest man in the world, classified these two types of decisions in his own way.

"Type 1" decisions are irreversible. They're the big, often monumental decisions that one can't take back. "Type 2" decisions are reversible, and while Bezos also warns against over-relying on them at the risk of being rash, used judiciously they allow the decision-maker more latitude to move quickly.

On the pitfalls of confusing the two, he states,

> As organizations get larger, there seems to be a tendency to use the heavy-weight Type 1

decision-making process on most decisions, including many Type 2 decisions. The end result of this is slowness, unthoughtful risk aversion, failure to experiment sufficiently, and consequently diminished invention. We'll have to figure out how to fight that tendency. And one-size-fits-all thinking will turn out to be only one of the pitfalls. We'll work hard to avoid it... and any other large organization maladies we can identify.

He's on our side regarding the action bias toward reversible decisions. It's what he sees as a hallmark of nimble, smart companies and is probably bemoaning the fact that every decision at a company as large as Amazon.com feels relatively heavyweight and irreversible.

There's a big caveat to making reversible decisions: they may inspire more possibilities and give you more flexibility, but they should still be based on facts—not unfounded projections, wishes, or excessive emotion. Reversible decisions work when they're realistic and supported by data or historical results. Even if you're making a decision that you can reverse out of, it's much easier to pivot inside and from a reversible decision if it's tethered to some kind of provable or established information.

As mentioned, decision-making alone is not a difficult task. But if we want to make the best decision possible, we can go ahead and use reversible decisions to learn exactly what you need to know.

MM #4: Seek "Satisfiction"

Use to achieve your priorities and ignore what doesn't matter.

Satisfiction *is* a made-up word, but not by me. I suppose that means it could be a real, official word.

The next mental model for decision-making focuses on increasing our speed by focusing only on what we need. In doing so, we will probably realize that we *need* far fewer things than we originally thought and that our desires are masquerading as needs.

The word *satisfice* is a combination of the words *satisfy* and *suffice*. It's a term that Herbert Simon coined in the 1950s, and it represents a handy alternative from those of us who seek to maximize the benefit we derive from a decision. As it turns out, most of us are split into two categories of decision-makers: *satisficers* and *maximizers*.

The maximizer is someone you might be familiar with. They want everything possible, and they'll try and try until they get it. They're picky to the point of being frustrating, and take all of their allotted time to make a decision, every time. Even then, they'll still second-guess themselves and regret their decision. The satisficer, on the other hand, can more accurately determine what really matters and focuses on those things. They get in and get out, and happily move on with their day.

Suppose that you are shopping for a new bike.

The maximizer would devote hours to researching their decision and evaluating as many options as possible. They would want to get the best one possible for their purposes and want to leave no stone unturned. They want 100% satisfaction, despite the law of diminishing returns—the poor return on investment from so many hours of research. The tires must be a certain brand, the frame must have a certain ratio of metal and plastic, and the brakes must be a certain color. Also, they want all of these things at a far below market price. This would make sense if the maximizer was a professional cyclist that frequently competed in international competition, but they are just an occasional weekend warrior.

The maximizer wants to make *perfect* decisions. This is typically an impossibility, and even if the maximizer feels they have finally reached this elusive goal (after hours of deliberation and introspection), they will probably quickly grow unhappy again because they won't be able to stop imagining other outcomes and greener pastures.

By contrast, the satisficer is just shooting to be satisfied and find an option that suffices for their purposes. They want something that works well enough to make them satisfied and pleased, but they don't need to feel overjoyed or ecstatic. Most anything will suffice so long as their general purpose and needs are taken care of. In other words, they aim for *good enough* and stop once they find that. What is a bike, really? It has two wheels, a sufficient frame, a comfortable enough seat, and working brakes. Most everything else is negotiable and not of interest to the satisficer.

This may seem like I'm downplaying how complex a bicycle can be, but I assure you that is not the case. The point being made is that this mental model recognizes but actively chooses to disregard most factors because they are not essential and thus don't serve the goals of mere satisfaction and sufficiency. They go too far above them.

Maximization represents a conundrum in our modern age, because while it is more possible than at any point in human history to get exactly what you want, there is also the paradox of choice, which makes it impossible to be satisfied. On a practical matter, there *are* decisions where we should strive to maximize our value. But they are extremely far and few between.

We are primed to make decisions on "just in case" or "that would be nice" or "wait until people see this" scenarios. We frequently waste time on what doesn't matter and what will never matter.

Most of our decisions are adequately made just by choosing an option that is reliable and honest. Suppose you are in a grocery store and you are trying to pick out the type of peanut butter you want. What should you shoot for here? Satisficing or maximizing? Clearly, you should just choose a peanut that falls within two or three of your general parameters and call it a day. Whatever net benefit the most optimal type of peanut butter brings to your life is likely not worth the extra effort it took to find it.

There is nothing to truly be gained by maximizing your choice in peanut butter, and this is a truth that applies to 99% of our daily decisions. Otherwise, we are constantly overwhelmed and waste our mental bandwidth on maximizing where it doesn't matter and where there are massive diminishing returns.

The concept of *satisfiction* is embodied in what is variously called the *37% rule* or the *secretary problem*. It supposes a fictional workplace that is interviewing for a new secretary position, and there are 100 candidates to be interviewed. Yet after the first 37, you will already understand the range of candidates and how qualified they may or may not be. In essence, you won't interview anyone that is different from what you have already seen; a maximized outlier is either extremely unlikely to appear or simply doesn't exist.

After seeing only 37% of the possible candidates, the rule instructs you to simply stop and make your choice then, because you've seen it all already and already know what you need to be both satisfied and feel that the candidate suffices. Of course, that is the zone of *satisfiction*. Strap on this mental model to save time and narrow down what you really want.

An easy method to seek satisfiction and not be unknowingly seduced into maximizing—spending way too much time on something that doesn't matter—is to set boundaries for yourself. This isn't about boundaries on research; rather, it's about boundaries on what you're looking for.

For example, if you go on a shopping trip for a new jacket, helpful boundaries are to only look at jackets that are made out of cotton, navy blue, and within a certain price range. It narrows your scope based on predetermined requirements. It allows you to quickly eliminate options while also knowing you will be satisficed at the end of the process.

A corollary to setting boundaries is to first decide upon a *default choice* up front if you can't decide within a set amount of time. The act of creating the default choice is important because you will have automatically selected something that fits your requirements or desires. You'll be happy in either case, in other words.

In many instances, the default is what you had in mind the entire time and where you were probably going to end up regardless of going through the motions and endless debate. You go through the mental exercise of choosing a "default" with the idea that you might end up there anyway.

MM #5: Stay Within 40–70%

Use to balance information with action.

A famous comedian has clever input on the matter of battling indecision: "My rule is that if you have someone or something that gets 70% approval, you just do it, 'cause here's what happens. The fact that other options go away immediately brings your choice to 80, because the pain of deciding is over."

This is surprisingly similar to what former U.S. Secretary of State Colin Powell has to say on the matter. Powell has a mental model about making decisions and coming to a point of action no sooner than necessary yet no longer than necessary.

He says that anytime you face a difficult decision, you should have *no less* than 40% and *no more* than 70% of the information you need to make that decision. In that range, you have enough information to make an informed choice but not so much intelligence that you lose your resolve and simply stay abreast of the situation. This makes you faster than more "informed" people and more informed than "fast" people. In a sense, it's the best of both worlds.

How did Powell come to this mental model on beating indecision? He felt that if you have less than 40% of the information you need, you're essentially shooting from the hip. You don't know quite enough to move forward and will probably make a lot of mistakes. You are sacrificing everything just for *speed*.

Conversely, if you chase down more over 70% of what you think you need (and it's unlikely that you'll truly need anything above this level), you will grow overwhelmed, slow, and uncertain. The opportunity may have passed you by and someone else may have beaten you by starting already. You are sacrificing everything just for *certainty*.

You are actually making the mistake of looking for 100% information and a foolproof plan where failure cannot exist. Many people who search for this don't realize that they are searching for something that doesn't exist and only acts to keep their own hands tied. Most engage in over-analysis and research that turns into procrastination, so they need to shoot for a zone of information that makes them uncomfortable.

But in that sweet spot between 40% and 70% information, you have more than enough to go on, and your intuition can fill in the gaps.

For this mental model, we can replace the word "information" with essentially anything else: 40–70% read or learned, 40–70% confidence, 40–70% planned, and so on. At the lower bounds, you are prepared enough to make at least a first step. Keep in mind that *while* the decision is being played out, you will also gain information, confidence, and knowledge that can bump you toward a higher degree of certainty. They aren't quite irreversible decisions, but taking action more quickly than not often has no downsides.

Utilize this mental model by intentionally consuming less information and even overgeneralizing—this means to not look at the subtleties of your options. Willfully ignore the gray area and don't rationalize or justify statements by saying "But..." or "That's not *always* true..."

The idea is to focus only on general, broad information and how that affects you. Suppose you are attempting to decide on a restaurant for dinner. How can you think more in black and white terms about something like this?

Overgeneralize your restaurant choices to how you would categorize them in a single phrase. Restaurant A is a place for burgers, despite the fact that there are five menu items that are not burgers. It doesn't matter—in black and white terms, it's a burger joint. Restricting the flow of information will naturally keep you within the 40–70% range and get you moving faster than ever.

MM #6: Minimize Regret

Use to consult the future you on decisions.

Once again, Jeff Bezos imparts a drop of decision-making wisdom into our lives. A guy who is one of the richest men in the world obviously has some tricks up his sleeve that got him to where he is.

This is the mental model of avoiding regrets and making *regret* the centerpiece of our decision-making calculus.

Jeff Bezos once found himself at a crossroads in his life in which he had to make some tough personal resolutions. He came up with a concept he termed the "regret minimization framework." ("Only a nerd would call" it that, Bezos joked.)

The concept of the regret minimization framework is quite basic. Bezos gave himself three very simple mental directives:

1. Project yourself to age 80.

2. Imagine yourself looking back on your life at that age, knowing that you want to feel as few regrets as possible.

3. Ask yourself, "In X number of years, will I regret taking this action (or *not* taking this action)?"

This mental model takes short-term emotional turmoil out of the equation and really forces perspective. When you project to 80 years old, you suddenly gain clarity on what matters and what does not. Regret is a powerful factor that might tell you more than all the positive sentiments in the world.

It also forces you to think about the future you actually want, as opposed to the one you are currently heading toward. First, you must determine what you want from your life, and then you can tailor your decisions toward it.

For Bezos, the answer was immediately obvious: if he didn't take the initiative and enter the Internet revolution, he'd regret it when he hit age 80. He'd regret not developing his idea for online book sales. He knew he would *not* regret failing, but he would *definitely* regret never giving it a shot.

When Bezos framed his dilemma that way, the decision was almost automatic. He quit his high-paying job at a hedge fund—even walking away from his annual bonus—moved to Seattle, and started running Amazon from his garage.

The Bezos mental model is applicable to almost any undertaking, minor or major. Think of something you always tell yourself you "mean to do," and usually *can* quite easily, but don't for some reason.

You want to start a blog but don't think you're a good enough writer. You want to run the Boston Marathon but don't think you can get in shape. A friend invites you to go skydiving, but the idea scares you to death. But your perceived lack of ability or courage is not the point. You can negotiate with yourself on those topics. But if you were to simply ask yourself, "In X number of years, will I regret taking this action (or *not* taking this action)," then you'd have a crystal-clear answer as to what you should do.

Let's take it to a grander, more Bezos-esque scale.

Suppose you have an idea to help build medical facilities in a faraway Third World country. The notion appeals to you in terms of impact, but you're anxious about the reality of being away from home for a year and living in a place where you might not understand the language, culture, or people. All of these factors are entirely separate from regret—will you regret never taking that chance? All signs point to yes. That means it is important to how you want to see yourself. That's almost always worth pursuing.

Takeaways:

- Mental models are blueprints we can use in various contexts to make sense of the world, interpret information correctly, and understand our context. They give us predictable outcomes. A recipe is the most basic form of mental model; each ingredient has its role, time, and place. However, a recipe is not applicable to anything outside the realm of food. Thus, we find ourselves in a position of wanting to learn a wide range of mental models (or latticework, as Charlie Munger puts it) to prepare ourselves for whatever may come our way. We can't learn ones for each individual scenario, but we *can* find widely applicable ones. In this chapter, we start with mental models for smarter and quicker decision-making.

- Mental Model #1: Address "Important"; Ignore "Urgent." These are entirely separate things that we often fuse together. Important is what truly matters, even if the payoff or deadline is not so immediate. Urgent only refers to the speed of response that is desired. You can easily use an Eisenhower Matrix to clarify your priorities and ignore urgent tasks, unless they so happen to also be important.

- Mental Model #2: Visualize All the Dominoes. We are a shortsighted species. We think only one step ahead in terms of consequences, and then we typically only limit it to our own consequences. We need to engage in second-order thinking and visualize all the dominos that could be falling. Without this, it can't be said that you are making a well-informed decision.

- Mental Model #3: Make Reversible Decisions. Most of them are; some of them aren't. But we aren't doing ourselves any favors when we assume that they are all irreversible, because it keeps us in indecision far too long. Create an action bias for reversible decisions, as there is nothing to lose and only information and speed to gain.

- Mental Model #4: Seek "Satisfiction." This is a mixture of satisfy and suffice, and it is aiming to make decisions that are good enough, adequate, and serve their purpose. This stands in stark contrast to those who wish to maximize their decisions with "just in case" and "that sounds nice" extras. Those who maximize are looking to make a perfect choice. This doesn't exist, so they are usually just left waiting.

- Mental Model #5: Stay Within 40–70%. This is Colin Powell's rule. Make a decision with no less than 40% of the information you need but no more than 70%. Anything less and you are just guessing; anything more and you are just wasting time. You can replace "information" with just about anything, and you will realize that this mental model is about encouraging quick yet informed decisions.

- Mental Model #6: Minimize Regret. Jeff Bezos developed what he calls the regret minimization framework. In it, he asks one to visualize themselves at age 80 and ask if they would regret making (or not making) a decision. This simplifies decisions by making them about one metric: regret.

Chapter 2. How to See More Clearly

Generally, binoculars come in handy. They provide focus and clarity to what would otherwise remain a blurry blob of color. They give us insight into a world that is completely foreign to us: the life of birds in a jungle canopy, the machinations of a squirrel looking for more acorns, or a gaseous structure of some of the planets in our solar system.

And yet, using binoculars completely blinds us to what is actually physically close to us and within our reach. When you use binoculars, you can't have it both ways: seeing the forest (big picture) and the trees (finer details) at the same time.

In general, seeing both is something that is ridiculously hard to accomplish. You have to beat your brain's tendency to jump to conclusions and fill in the blanks into submission, as well as deal with the fact that when you focus your attentions in one place, something else will inevitably be overlooked. Even if we're extremely attentive, we can't always rely on what we see and hear to give us a complete picture of what is happening.

Sometimes we don't get complete information—there's always something we *can't* see or hear that might be driving events. Sometimes we rely on the stories of other people who might have a hidden agenda for explaining events the way they do. And we also have our *own* inherent biases and beliefs that may color what we see to the point where our judgment becomes inaccurate or faulty.

Humans don't naturally think or see objectively. Once we reach this realization, we can better act toward preventing it. This chapter addresses perceiving the world for what it actually *is*, something that even the most discerning of us struggle with from day to day. These mental models help you see through the distractions and false realities of everyday existence so you can get as close to the core truth as you possibly can.

It comes in handy more often than you might expect. For instance, there is a saying that if you wish to move to a new location, you should visit it in all seasons or at least during the extreme seasons of summer and winter. It wouldn't be wise to form your opinion and make your decision based on the five-day stretch you visited, where it happened to have the best weather possible for the past 10 years.

Any given situation or object, no matter how fixed or permanent it might seem, is subject to change with surrounding conditions or events. If you've only visited Chicago in the summertime, you might be led to believe that it's a humid and hot place, which it is—in summer. But as anyone who's endured a Chicago blizzard can tell you, it's a wildly different place in winter. Somewhere in there are a few days of moderate, pleasant weather, but if that's your expectation, you are going to be sorely disappointed.

When it comes to information, less is *not* more. It can be easy to feel overburdened and overwhelmed by facts, to say nothing of others' interpretations and explanations of all those facts. But there really is no substitute for having as much intelligence and knowledge as you can gather.

This overall mindset encourages you to obtain as much information about a situation or topic in a variety of different backgrounds, environments, and conditions as you possibly can. Having all this information prevents you from making snap judgments, blind assumptions, and inaccurate projections—all of which you need to avoid to make better decisions.

To develop a broader, more complete viewpoint of all situations, we'll break down this overall mental model into three more specific templates.

MM #7: Ignore "Black Swans"

Use to understand how outliers shouldn't actually change your thinking.

Until nearly the 18th century, people in the Western world—which at the time basically referred to Europe—believed that all swans were white. Their reasoning was simple: they'd never seen anything *besides* white swans. Absent swans of any other shade or color, they had no reason to believe swans of other colors existed. It never even crossed their minds.

But in 1697, Dutch explorer Willem de Vlamingh traveled to Australia, a site that Europeans didn't start visiting until 1606; it was still a relatively new frontier for them. While exploring what's now known as the Swan River near the present-day city of Perth in Western Australia, de Vlamingh and his crew saw what no European had ever seen before: black swans—*lots* of them. News of their discovery had a strong impact, rewriting quite a few tenets of their belief systems about zoology that were based on the principle that all swans were white.

Goodbye centuries of supposed knowledge, hello indisputable evidence of being incorrect. What if swans could be all colors of the rainbow? What does this mean for humans? What are the far-reaching implications of discovering a black swan?

Statistician Nassim Nicholas Taleb adapted this bit of history to form the "black swan" theory. Taleb uses the black swan as a metaphor to describe unpredictable events that create a massive change in perception, perspective, and understanding. And yet, in his definition, a black swan event is something that should *not* change perception or accepted knowledge because it is such an anomalous outlier. It may simply create awareness of possibilities, but most black swan events don't deserve to be accounted for in everyday life. Maybe it just means that swans come in white and black, and belief systems on zoology don't need to be thrown out the window.

As a brief example, the knowledge that a lightning bolt struck a tree nearby can be frightening, and it might encourage you to equip some houses with grounding rods.

But should such a one-time event influence the way you live your life, staying indoors whenever it starts to rain, carrying a metal shield around with you at all times, or moving to a part of the world that has little to no rain like the desert? Does it mean we should all move underground to live as mole people? No, this event shouldn't have such influence.

On a global scale, events like the fall of the Berlin Wall, assassination of a public figure, and the tragedy of 9/11 could be considered black swan events. On a more personal level, they could include a factory suddenly closing, a local company being bought out by a major conglomerate, parents divorcing, a house being burgled— anything that disrupts and upends our placement or personal views. There is an impact to be sure, but how much should we truly account for these outliers?

As unnerving, drastic, and cataclysmic as black swan events might be, their overall importance to one's belief system or worldview *can* be overestimated. Human nature being what it is, one might even try to qualify a black swan event and excuse it in retrospect: "Well, when you really think about it, all the signs were there and we should have seen it coming." Such a viewpoint tends to rewrite our understanding and belief system.

And that's a problem, because no matter how devastating or overwhelming a black swan event might be, it's *still* an irregularity or aberration. Black swan events are not "the norm." Many of them don't happen more than once or twice in a lifetime. But their shocking, sometimes catastrophic natures can make one alter, distort, or overturn one's knowledge, beliefs, and world outlook. A black swan event's power can be devastating—but does it warrant the importance we ascribe to it?

Taleb says there are three elements to a black swan event.

It's a big surprise. The happening or event in question must be completely unforeseeable. There can be no way the observer could have seen it coming in advance.

It has a major effect. The black swan event must have some sort of fateful or immense outcome, whether it's physical, structural, or emotional.

People attempt to rationalize it after it happens. After the black swan event takes place for the first time, people affected by it might root around for "signs they missed" or try to explain in retrospect how people *should* have expected the event to happen in the first place.

That third element is where one runs into trouble. A black swan event can be so all-encompassing, indeed traumatic, that it could force a wholesale reformation of one's beliefs or personal policies. But a black swan event is still an outlier, especially when it's a random bolt from the blue that couldn't have possibly been accounted for. To ascribe too much importance to a black swan event, to let it account for wide-sweeping changes that weren't there when it happened, is at heart nonsensical.

This mental model is about looking past the gravity of a black swan event, zooming out, and seeing the whole picture. Don't let the possibility of more lightning make you move to the desert. Catering to black swan events will come at the detriment of everything else in your belief systems, as well as large opportunity costs.

When you are faced with big events— business or personal—allow room to consider that it may very well be a black swan event that, while important, is not very informative or indicative of anything at all. Don't organize your entire strategy around the likelihood of a black swan event; unless you work for the Federal Emergency Management Agency (FEMA), disasters are not going to be an everyday part of your existence.

Let yourself *think* about worst-case scenarios. But then bring yourself back to reality. Is this event likely to occur again? How much of an outlier was it? Can we reasonably even do anything about it? Should it change the way we act if it is inevitable from time to time? If lightning will strike a few times a decade, is it worth it to retrofit your entire operation and home to account for that? In other words, should you stop driving cars because you heard an acquaintance got into an accident?

Smart planning will always seek to understand risk factors, but it must also accurately them. Life is full of risks— we take them every day when we cross the road. But life must go on. You shouldn't live your life in fear of a black swan event, but you can and should simply put a few moments of consideration into how they might happen and what they might require you to do.

If we zoom out a bit on black swan events, you'll realize that we are trying to find a predictable pattern in what is actually a random set of events. This is known as the gambler's fallacy, named for sentiments such as rolling a pair of dice and feeling that you must eventually roll a seven because it has *been a while* or *you're due*.

Never mind the fact that this is not statistically or probabilistically sound; you are attempting to create order in something impossible to have control over. The gambler's fallacy is the notion that just because X happened, Y should happen, X shouldn't happen, or X should happen again. More often than not, these events are all independent of each other, and this should guide your decision-making to be less biased.

The gambler's fallacy is representative of a broader phenomenon known as *apophenia*, which is the human tendency to see patterns and connections through random data points, usually also coinciding with *too few* data points. This is why people see rabbits in clouds and elaborate scenes through inkblot tests.

MM #8: Look for Equilibrium Points

Use to find real patterns in data and not be fooled.

The second piece of the general mental model of visiting a city in all seasons, or simply seeing the whole picture, has to do with what are known as *diminishing returns.*

This is an economic principle that describes how an increase in resources doesn't always correspond to an increase in the outcome you want. In plain terms, this means that where you might be ecstatic to eat one donut, the amount of joy you feel will drastically decrease as you get to donut number ten. There is no linear relationship between input and output.

What we get back from our efforts is a decrease of what we were seeking; there is a natural rate of decay for where the more resources we put into something, the less we get out of it. Sometimes it is even an inverse relationship (the more resource, the less output).

The mistake we often make is to base our assumptions, predictions, projections, or information in general on the assumption that input will always correspond with output. We must look past shiny beginnings that are misrepresentative and wait for equilibrium, because that's what we should draw conclusions from. While there isn't necessarily a predictable rate that diminishing returns follows, the existence of it is predictable in general. If you don't account for it, you are being myopic and not seeing the world for what it is.

If you are learning how to play a new instrument, you will make leaps and bounds at the beginning because it is all new. It's easy to go from not knowing how a piano works to playing "Twinkle Twinkle Little Star," and yet that represents a mathematically infinite amount of improvement. However, this progress will rapidly slow down, and you will have to put in increasing amounts of effort to keep improving. How will you fare when you must constantly struggle? That's the equilibrium where your true rate of improvement lies.

The law of diminishing returns encourages us to look for equilibrium points to accurately assess and learn information. Just like with black swan events, you can't base your judgments off outliers or skewed information.

But equilibrium points also apply to how much effort we should expend toward an outcome.

More often than not, when we decide to put more "input" into our work, something else tends to get lost. If you try reading 900 words a minute, you will lose comprehension and understanding, which is far more valuable to the overall task of reading. If you try learning the piano too intensely, you will burn out and start hating it. If you try to study for nine hours straight, chances are you won't remember much. Not recognizing the law of diminishing returns will usually hurt you.

So this mental model has two uses: first, to more accurately analyze information about others; second, to know where your own equilibrium points are and when you should rethink how much effort you are putting in for the number of results you are getting.

This doesn't mean that your efforts are worthless—in general, if you *don't* work toward something, you won't get anything at all. But by the same token, working harder and harder toward something doesn't mean your rewards will increase in proportion to your efforts.

For the answer, we're going to have to go all the way back to Mother Goose: be like Goldilocks and find a zone of satisfaction.

In the off chance that you need a refresher, Goldilocks was the fabled girl who went into the home of three bears while they were out and about and started sampling all their food and furnishings. She found the father bear's chair "too hard," the mother bear's chair as "too soft," and the baby bears chair to be "just right." Other variations have Goldilocks being picky about the size of the bowls and the taste of the food.

If you can overlook the fact that Goldilocks seemed to think there's nothing wrong with breaking and entering into a wild animal's home, the moral of the story is that there is a certain zone of satisfaction where your input and effort provide an acceptable amount of satisfaction or outcome. If you expend too many resources and effort, you move out of the zone—too little outcome. If you expend too little, you move out of the zone—too little outcome. If you expect too much or too few results, you also move out of the zone.

Seeing the world clearly requires having a clear understanding of cause and effect.

MM #9: Wait for the Regression to the Mean

Use to find real patterns in data and not be fooled. (Yes, again)

As mentioned in the discussion of black swan events, sometimes we mistake an "extreme" or extraordinary event for something we need to plan around, but more often than not the event is just an "outlier" that doesn't really signify how things are. Even if a big event or happening shakes up our immediate surroundings, it shouldn't be automatically used to assume a "new reality." More likely than not, the black swan event won't (or at least shouldn't) have a total, utter change to your daily experience or beliefs.

Related to that is the idea of "regression to the mean." For those of you (like myself) for whom math isn't exactly second nature, the "mean" essentially represents something akin to an "average": a sort of midpoint that indicates a sort of normalcy, a kind of "typical" value. In our definition, "the mean" means the usual or most common status of a given situation.

For example, consider a week of family meals. Probably at least five times every week the family eats at home. On the weekend or on special occasions, the family might go to a restaurant and have a more expensive meal that they don't have to cook. That's an outlier, though. Usually, they'll eat at home, and that's "the mean."

Maybe one week they'll go to a really expensive restaurant. Perhaps they'll go on a cruise for a week and eat every single meal in a luxury ocean liner. But that's not something they can sustain every single day. *Eventually* they're going to get back to their usual routine of eating at home without too many bells and whistles. That's their usual practice—the mean—and at *some* point, they're going to "regress" and settle back into it.

Take the common example of how obsessive and optimistic a couple is when they first get together. This is known as the *honeymoon period*, and it is imbued with new relationship energy. But it would be a mistake to assume that this rate of love and obsession is truly representative of the relationship. There will soon be a regression to a normal and sustainable rate of *love*—the *real* rate of love that can be expected. That's when you know if a relationship is more than a cocktail of hormones.

If you are a basketball player and you have a long history of making shots at a 40% rate, that's your mean. If you start making shots at a 50% rate, it doesn't mean that you're suddenly a better player, because eventually, you will just regress back to the mean. Outliers that appear to be patterns or deviations can fool us.

Regression to the mean happens with every aspect of our lives. If you start dating someone new, your apartment is going to be clean and your hygiene will probably be immaculate. And yet, this doesn't represent a true change in behavior on your side. As the relationship grows longer and more comfortable, you will regress to the mean in your cleanliness and hygiene. If there was no basis for a change in the first place, eventually things will simply get back to normal.

A slightly more *scientific* explanation of regression to the mean, as originally conceived by British statistician Sir Francis Galton, is that in any sequence of events that are affected by different conditions or variables—such as environment, emotions, and plain old luck—extraordinary events are usually followed by more ordinary, typical ones. So when an aberrant, deviant, or untypical event happens, it's much more likely that it won't happen again in a patterned way. Rather, the pattern that's much more probable to return is "the usual."

This mental model encourages you to simply wait and see. If something extreme occurs, wait to see the recovery. If something unexpected or unpredicted happens, wait to see the aftermath. If something appears to be trending, wait to see what happens after it stops trending (for example, the seeming rise of bellbottom pants every couple of decades).

Remember, without an actual basis for a change or extreme event, the mean will always do what Arnold Schwarzenegger uttered in the Terminator, "I'll be back."

Let the entire cycle play out and assess *all* of the information you'll encounter during that time. Don't make any sudden moves or change of plan after the occurrence of the big, abnormal event. By being patient and waiting for events to return to their normal state, you'll get a much better sense of how the situation has been changed. Statistically speaking, it will probably not be that much at all.

Visiting a city in all four seasons may be difficult, time-consuming, and tedious, but these three mental models are just the beginning of how to properly collect information and be unswayed by seductive yet incorrect perspectives. "Black swan" events, equilibrium points, and regressions to the mean all obscured our thoughts because they are more emotional than realistic.

An essential aspect of seeing the whole picture is to understand when things are and are not connected or related. We have a tendency to fabricate a cause and effect relationship where there is none.

There are clear psychological reasons for this. Uncertainty scares people. At least some of the time, we want to know what's going to happen in the near and distant future. When we can't figure it out with hard evidence or data, we use our instincts, gut feelings or "hunches."

Sometimes it's true those hunches are on the money and can save a lot of trouble. But more often than not, those hunches don't amount to real information and tend to be a waste of our analytical resources. Even the ones that turn out to be correct are more similar to a stopped clock being correct twice a day by default. Everyone has their lucky guesses.

If we have this tendency, we might as well try to ensure that it is as accurate and clear as possible. While there's no surefire way to accurately predict everything that's going to happen in the future, there are several mental models we can use to establish the likelihood of certain events happening—or, more helpfully, prepare us for whatever results emerge. They don't allow us to predict the future, but they do encourage us to analyze the chain of events and incorporate probabilistic thinking into our daily lives.

These models rely on objectivity and logic instead of subjective emotions and intuition. They also help us understand when our analyses of certain situations and correlated events are working, or whether we're making associations and links between events that really don't have any relation to each other. The goal with these models is to evaluate and plan for the future in a more precise and practical way.

MM #10: What Would Bayes Do (WWBD)?

Use to calculate probabilities and predict the future based on real events.

We now step out of the shadow of trying to glean predictions from insufficient information. This next mental model is all about what we should *actually* be using to try to draw conclusions.

Despite the fact that we stink at predicting the future, we try anyway. Sometimes, when we crave a sense of assuredness about how future events are going to unfold, we rely on "experts" in the media who fearlessly go on television and radio shows to unveil their learned opinions about what's going to happen tomorrow, next week, or next year. If there is a small piece of information, you can bet that someone is going to make an erroneous prediction based on it.

The problem is that those famous people are not that much better at predicting the future than we are. Think of all the huge, unforeseen events that have taken place over the last quarter century—chances are, the biggest ones are the events nobody saw coming, least of all those onscreen analysts whose jobs seemingly depend on their predictions. They're good for ratings and to make people feel at least temporarily better about the future.

But they're usually wrong, regardless of what side of the thought spectrum they're on. Trying to understand what is going to happen in the near future becomes a game of salacious guessing rather than sincerely trying to forecast.

The one thing that this mental model supports is what they rarely take into account.

And that represents a bigger problem we have as aware human beings: sometimes it becomes difficult for us to filter out the "noise" and focus in on the objective "signals" that reveal more of the truth about certain situations, including the future.

In fact, that provided Nate Silver, arguably the most famous statistician in the world today, with the title of his 2012 book: *The Signal and the Noise*. Silver's book addresses why so many media fortune-tellers (including, sometimes, him) make such erroneous predictions. One of the most common problems, Silver maintains, is their continuing inability to differentiate between factors that are truly important to observe and the "noisy" non-factors that keep getting in the way of objective analysis.

Although there's no proven model that's going to provide a foolproof formula for predicting the future (obviously), Silver brings up a theorem that can at least provide some clarity about events in the world that can at least lead to better comprehension of our world—which *may* lead to, if not a higher rate of successful prediction, a state of being better informed and able to handle reality.

This template is known as *Bayes' Theorem*, named after the 18th-century mathematician Thomas Bayes. *Encyclopedia Britannica* defines Bayes' Theorem as "a means for revising predictions in light of relevant evidence, also known as conditional probability or inverse probability."

Jargon aside, it's a formula for predicting what might happen *if* other meaningful events have occurred. Bayes' Theorem deals with *probability*, because of course nothing is certain or inevitable. But it's helped companies like Google and IBM experiment with probability and generating ideas, and it's also proven beneficial to sports bettors and those in predictive sciences like climate science. Simply, if A occurs, and it is related to B, then you can generate a tangible probability.

There's an actual formula to Bayes' Theorem, and while I'm not eager to give you a math problem to figure out, it's helpful to at least know what the formula looks like:

$$P(A|B) = \frac{P(A) \times P(B|A)}{P(B)}$$

The probability of A occurring if B has already occurred is written as P(A|B). A is what you are solving for and what you are trying to predict.

The probability of B occurring if A has already occurred is written as *P(B|A).*

The probability of A occurring on its own without B is written as P(A).

The probability of B occurring on its own without A is written as P(B).

Take a moment to process exactly what is being quantified. A percentage is created, where you are essentially weighing probabilities based on what has and hasn't happened. It's actually much easier to illustrate with an example.

All you need are three numbers, and you are able to solve for a rough probability of a future occurrence. You need the probabilities of event A, event B, and event B if A has occurred. Tornados are rare (1% probability), but heavy winds are fairly common (10%) and 90% of tornados cause heavy winds. You want to know the probability of there being a tornado if there are heavy winds. The equation is this:

Probability (tornado|heavy winds) = **_P(tornado) × P(heavy winds|tornado)_**

P(heavy winds)

Probability (tornado|heavy winds) = **_1% × 90%_**

10%
Probability (tornado|heavy winds) = 9%

So the probability of a tornado when there is heavy wind is 9%. As you can see, all you need are three figures, and then it's really just plugging the numbers into Bayes' formula. This figure ends up being more rooted in reality than what any expert could tell you.

You can use it in any number of circumstances, big to small, insignificant to life-changing. Bayes' Theorem is powerful because it allows us to take actually quantify uncertainty and certainty with just a small number of variables. It mimics real-life analysis in a way that we typically only use in hindsight, and the information it provides helps us ground ourselves in reality. Numbers don't lie, after all. The formula allows us to cut through the noise of what masquerades as impactful and ties it to something real and important.

So in your further quest for clear thinking, utilize the mental model and ask, "What would Bayes do?" He'd stop making assumptions, focus on what is really happening in real-life, and spit out a probability to help you make decisions and evaluate. Inherent in Bayesian thinking is that you must keep updating your probabilities based on new information and that while everything is uncertain, it is more certain than you think.

MM #11: Do It Like Darwin

Use to seek real, honest truth in a situation.

Seeing clearly also means seeing both sides of the table. For that, we have a mental model brought to you by none other than Charles Darwin himself.

Charles Darwin, the naturalist whose theories on evolution and the development of species had wide-ranging effects on scientific study that persist today, was apparently not a genius. He wasn't especially good at math. He didn't have the quick thinking often attributed to geniuses. Charlie Munger once said he thought that if Darwin attended Harvard in 1986, he probably would have graduated around the middle of the pack.

Biologist E.O. Wilson estimated that Darwin's IQ would have been around 130 or so—high, but not quite the level (140) where the word "genius" starts getting mentioned. He was obviously very bright, but the point is that he possessed a different skill that led him to his accomplishments.

Darwin was *relentless* about learning.

He devoured information about all the topics he was interested in pursuing. He hoarded facts and was hyper-diligent about taking notes. His ability to hold attention was legendary, and his work ethic was tireless. Darwin's thinking was purposely slow because he was so fastidiously detail-oriented. He believed that to have any authority on any topic, one needed to develop deep expertise on it, and expertise doesn't happen overnight (or in a month or in a year).

And here's where he deviated to the point that we want to use him as a mental model: Darwin's method was so all-encompassing that he even gave deep attention to information that countered or challenged his own theories. This approach forms the backbone of his *golden rule* as he expressed in his autobiography and the mental model we attribute to him. The basic guideline of Darwin's golden rule was to be more than just open to contradicting or opposing ideas—indeed, Darwin gave it his fullest attention:

> I had, also, during many years, followed a golden rule, namely, that whenever a published fact, a new observation or

thought came across me, which was opposed to my general results, to make a memorandum of it without fail and at once; for I had found by experience that such facts and thoughts were far more apt to escape from memory than favorable ones.

Darwin completely immersed himself in evidence or explanations that went against his findings because he was aware that the human mind is inclined to dispose of those contrary views. If he didn't investigate them as fully as he could, he'd be likely to forget them, and that created mental dishonesty. Darwin knew that his own instinctual thinking could be a hindrance to finding the truth as much as it could help, and he established a way to ensure he wasn't missing out on any information.

Darwin handled all this conflicting information responsibly.

He genuinely considered material that might have disproved his assertions and took pains to fully absorb every single scenario, anomaly, and exception to his theories. He didn't filter out information that didn't support his beliefs; he was utterly immune to confirmation bias. More than anything else, Darwin didn't want to be careless in finding the truth—he knew that a half-cocked assertion solely intended to persuade others without much thought was intellectually dishonest. Doing so required more time and effort on his part, but he was committed.

Of course, the Darwinian golden rule calls back to intellectual honesty and the maxim "strong opinions but held lightly." It assumes intellectual *humility*: being unattached to any stances or theories and simply following the evidence.

Uniquely, Darwin forces a dialogue of skepticism back onto himself instead of onto others in defensiveness. He dispassionately questioned himself in a way that we reserve for others. He would direct questions inward, such as, *What do you know? Are you sure? Why are you sure? How can it be proved? What potential errors could you have made? Where is this conflicting view coming from and why?* As you can imagine, it takes quite a bit of self-discipline to constantly double-check yourself.

Darwin accurately realized that if you hold the belief that everyone *else* is wrong, you're in trouble. Unfortunately, the simplest explanation is that *you* are the one who's wrong.

Darwin knew he had to comprehend the arguments *against* his own theories more thoroughly than someone who made those arguments. He probably would have been a very poor salesman. This mental model is certainly not how most people think, and that's the beauty of it.

As an extension of Darwin's golden rule and embracing both sides of an issue, you must be willing to blindly *follow the evidence.* Wherever it points is where you go. It's likely that you'll have a narrative in your head beforehand, but it's something you have to put completely to the side.

You might find real evidence that supports your point of view—great. But you'll also find evidence that you don't necessarily want to face, the kind that offers cogent and reasonable arguments against your position. Even people who have devoted themselves to fearless truth-seeking might bristle at this kind of evidence and try to avoid or ignore it.

What would Darwin say? That's exactly the kind of evidence you should need to follow and follow to its utmost. It's a deceptively simple task—if you can resist the psychological discomfort it causes.

Treat all the evidence you receive by the same standards of reliability. All of it needs to pass the same sniff test. You must be circumspect of all evidence, and this means tending toward high-*quality* information more than high *quantities* of information.

Overall, Darwin's mental model is about one thing over all else: truth. Out of all the models in this book, this might be the one most neglected and abused of all.

MM #12: Think With System 2

Use to think analytically versus emotionally.

The last mental model about thinking clearly and not being fooled has to do with how our brain functions—on its own, not in a way that we would usually prefer.

The brain is a wonder of biology. However, just like the rest of us, it prefers to save its energy and take the path of least resistance whenever possible. To do so, the brain downgrades some of its processes and downright skips others so it can conserve energy. This means that it's always seeking shortcuts so we don't have to think through every last thing. In reality, the brain ends up cutting corners, and this leads us to make mistakes on a daily basis.

Over the years, this has led to two biological systems of thought—one focused on speed and conservation of energy and the other focused on accuracy and analysis. This is something we must be vigilant about, especially when we are introduced to new information or concepts. The brain would rather save energy for dangerous situations, but little does it realize that it can actually cause them by flawed thinking.

This concept was popularized by professor Daniel Kahneman in his seminal book *Thinking Fast & Slow*. Through a series of experiments, Kahneman developed a model that explains the separate processes the brain uses to absorb and react to various bits of information, imaginatively titled *System 1 thinking* and *System 2 thinking*.

System 1 is "fast" thinking. This mode is automatic and instinctive. It's what we use when we happen upon a situation that we're familiar with and don't need to process that much, like recognizing a friend, riding a bicycle, or doing single-digit math calculations. Since it's intuitive, System 1 thinking is also associated with emotional reactions, like crying or laughing when seeing an old photograph. The fight-or-flight instinct fits right into System 1 thinking.

The main facet of System 1 thinking is effortlessness. It doesn't require anything in the way of analysis or consideration, instead using a framework of associations that we've already experienced time and time again. System 1 is a series of mental shortcuts—called *heuristics*—that help us decode situations very quickly (more on those soon). And because there's little time or effort used in System 1 thinking, it expends less energy and isn't terribly exhausting. You're not going to need a list of pros and cons to make decisions with System 1. Although System 1 is faster, it's aimed at doing the *fast* thing versus the *right* thing.

You may have heard the term *cognitive bias* before—they result precisely from System 1 taking over.

System 2, on the other hand, is "slow" thinking. This is the mental model that we are seeking to use more, as it is much more contemplative and analytical. It's used for any situation that requires more mental labor and effort. System 2 is used for decision-making in events that could result in high consequences, like choosing a college, buying a new car, or quitting your job.

You also use System 2 when you're doing something that needs more focus or effort, like driving through a foggy night, striving to hear someone speak in a noisy room, trying to recall a conversation you had a few weeks ago, or learning a complex school subject that's new to you.

Where System 1 thinking is fluent and instinctive, System 2 thinking is the opposite: it's deliberate, conscious, and methodical. System 1 thinking is the proverbial skydiver, where System 2 thinking is the proverbial cautious lawyer. System 2 needs time and labor to process new information—and as a result, it uses more brain energy and can be tiring or draining. That flustered and fatigued feeling you might get while studying or reading a book isn't because you can't understand it or are bored; it's an actual biological imperative.

You're using up your System 2 energy, and that's why we always default to System 1. That's a shame because it makes us susceptible to accepting things at first glance, not thinking skeptically, being more gullible, and overall thinking in faulty ways. It also makes us impulsive and rash without considering consequences or implications. Overall, we become more primal and *dumber*.

For things you encounter on a regular basis or have deep familiarity with, it's great—this is where System 1 thinking shines. If you have a plethora of experience with it, it can indeed help you make a good decision. It's also obviously useful when dangerous or fearful elements are present, as System 1 thinking springs you into action where analysis and careful consideration would leave you dead.

There's a time and place for both System 1 and 2 thinking, but in the absence of dangerous, life and death situations, System 2 is preferable for clear thinking.

We can't use it all the time because it would be impractical and too time-consuming. But more importantly, it's plain exhausting, especially if you have to keep forcing yourself to do it. In truth, this should perhaps be the first mental model you should invoke when you realize you need to remain unbiased and think clearly. Being stuck in System 1 will limit just about every deeper train of thought you could have.

Takeaways:

- Seeing and thinking clearly is not something we instinctually do. Humans are all about survival, pleasure, avoiding pain, food, sex, and sleep. Everything else that we would consider a higher pursuit tends to come second, at least in our brains. Thus, mental models to ensure that we are thinking clearly are of the utmost importance. The world usually looks different at second glance.

- Mental Model #7: Ignore "Black Swans." This is the first mental model that specifically warns against our tendency to jump to conclusions based on imperfect, skewed, or incomplete information. A black swan event is an entirely unpredictable event that comes out of nowhere. In doing so, it skews all data and beliefs, and people start to take the black swan into account as a new normal. But these are just outliers that should be ignored.

- Mental Model #8: Look for Equilibrium Points. This mental model is about noticing trends in progress. When you first start something, you go from zero to one—that's an infinite rate of progress. Then you go from one to two, two to three, and so on, and the rate of progress slows, and the returns start diminishing. Somewhere around there is an equilibrium point that truly represents what the average mean will be. Don't make the mistake of not waiting for it.

- Mental Model #9: Wait for the Regression to the Mean. This is the final mental model about seeing the whole picture in terms of information. A change without a *reason* for the change is not really a change; it's just a deviation. As such, it doesn't represent what will continue to happen in the future. A regression to the mean is when things settle back down and resume what they were doing before—this is representative of reality.

- Mental Model #10: What Would Bayes Do (WWBD)? Funnily enough, the previous three mental models were about our flawed attempts to draw conclusions and predict the future. Bayes' Theorem is something that actually does allow us to draw conclusions about the future: based on probabilities and taking into account events that have already occurred. All you need are the rough probabilities of three elements to plug into the Bayes' formula, and you will come to a more accurate conclusion than so-called experts. This is basic probabilistic thinking.

- Mental Model #11: Do It Like Darwin. Darwin apparently was not a genius, but he did have one trait that set him apart from others: his undying devotion to truth. In doing so, he developed his golden rule (and our mental model) of giving equal weight and attention to arguments and opinions that opposed his own. Instead of growing defensive when presented with something that opposed him, he grew critical and skeptical toward himself. This radical open-mindedness puts aside confirmation bias and ego.

- Mental Model #12: Think With System 2. We each have two systems of thought, courtesy of Daniel Kahneman: System 1 and System 2. System 1 focuses on speed and efficiency of thought, while System 2 focuses on accuracy and depth of thought. System 2 is smart, while System 1 is dumb. System 1 does more harm than good, but unfortunately, it is the one we default to because it is easier. Gain awareness of the difference between the two; acknowledge System 1, then try to jump immediately to System 2.

Chapter 3. Eye-Opening Problem-Solving

Everyone's got problems.

Problems are interruptions of one's life—obstacles. Sometimes they are tiny and vanish in a second, and other times we can't cope with them and they force us to reevaluate our entire lives. No matter the magnitude, in one way or another, we cope with them. We've gotten this far in our lives, and this doesn't happen from avoiding everything challenging that comes our way. Over time, we've found solutions through brute force and massive amounts of attempts, or even lucky guessing.

There's probably a better way. There are many ways to fry a fish, yet sometimes the fish turns out consistently tasty, while other times the fish is barely edible. It turns out there are probably some effective, tried and true methods for general problem-solving, and it would serve you well to understand them.

This chapter introduces some mental models geared toward solving problems and providing solutions for whatever is in front of you. They provide exact steps in thinking that will help you focus and make sense of the chaos that problems raise. To effectively solve problems, one needs to be a bit innovative and look for new ways to tackle them. The same tools and thought patterns won't work for everything, and mental models prove especially well-suited to solving problems because they provide literal guidelines about how to probe for solutions.

They're methodical and systematic in a way that we either find too tedious or can't quite organize. Suppose you have a 500-piece puzzle, but all the pieces are exactly the same color. You might be able to finish this puzzle eventually, but it'll be a struggle because you have no structure on how to start. Most people would start with the borders, the sky, or some other recognizable milestone. These mental models are like a template for how the puzzle fits together.

Sure, most problems can be solved through ramming your head into a wall enough times that cracks begin to form, but we can strive for more than that.

One of the major issues we must first address is the matter of our limited perspective. We spend 24 hours a day within our own heads. Once in a while we break to take in other information, but generally speaking, our own opinions are the ones that we hear the most. We also probably interact mostly with people who share our opinions, and thus we find ourselves in an echo chamber of sorts. This all leads us to consider our opinions to be rightful, correct, and important. You can probably see the issues starting to form already.

It's important to have a certain amount of trust and confidence in your inner voice, but it's not the only valid perspective that exists, and sometimes it may not even be correct. The first few mental models are about how to step outside your own head and see a situation and thus problem as clearly as possible. You may realize that a solution was in front of you the whole time, but your perspective wouldn't allow for it or acknowledge it.

Outside of problem-solving, it's just a good mental model for life because it forces a certain amount of empathy for others. When you can step into other people's perspectives, you are encouraged to ask how it came about, how it's reasonable to them, and why it all fits together. Most people are not acting out of evil, nor do they wish to oppose you just to spite you. Similarly, everyone feels that they are the hero in their story (including you), so it can be revealing to understand how *you* can appear to be the villain in a story. This is yet another habit that we are not accustomed to on a consistent basis.

Thus, it's vital to explore viewpoints that don't necessarily agree with our own.

No matter how firmly one might think they feel or how much they know, there's really no way for them to verify that their viewpoint is the only right one. Even the most respected and trusted world leaders have advisers who act as sounding boards for their ideas. They realize that their experience is only a portion of the greater situation; without knowing how other parties feel, they're only able to see a small part of the problem (if any at all).

When it comes to our own, less earth-shaking issues, it's still equally as important to understand other points of view—especially those that are most challenging or contrary to our most treasured thoughts, no matter how difficult it may be to hear them. The mental models in this section will help you develop and maintain the kind of receptiveness to other positions that you need to make effective decisions and solve problems.

MM #13: Peer Review Your Perspectives

Use to understand the consensus view and why you might differ.

Peer reviews are conducted in many disciplines. They're most commonly associated with scholarly publications, but almost any endeavor—professional, scientific, or otherwise—has some form of peer review as part of its operations. As the name implies, a peer review is an evaluation of your work conducted by other people in your field. Other like-minded colleagues within your area of study or expertise review your work and offer feedback and suggestions in advance of submission. Often, this devolves into people viciously trying to rip your research apart and find flaws where they can. But actually, the more vicious, the more helpful it can be.

The goal of peer reviews is to guard against inaccuracies or omissions in a final work and to offer alternative viewpoints that could help make the results clearer, more relevant, or precise. Examiners review your premise, your methodology, your analysis, your conclusion, and everything that links those things together. This scientific and methodical approach is the best way to put your perspectives under scrutiny and make them bulletproof—or at least informed.

The best peer reviews leave no stones unturned and make sure the originator is presenting work that's been subjected to as much examination as possible. You'll come away knowing your weaknesses, strengths, and where you generally stand.

While this may not be very practicable on a daily basis, the purpose can be carried out in a few ways. If you have an opinion or perspective, that's one data point. What about trying to gather three more? And then what about trying to gather two that are opposed to yours and present different and novel angles?

You can gather information, intelligence, and other points of view in as complete a manner as possible to reinforce or fine-tune your thoughts or plans and help you make better decisions in the process of problem-solving. When you can find the consensus opinion, you can then gauge whether you align with it, or determine why and how you differ. Often this will open up new avenues of thought and exploration.

A specific application of this mental model is called *triangulation.* It's based on, among other things, the military practice of confirming a certain location by drawing lines from three different points of origin to form a "triangle" to it. The more data points available, the more sides the triangle gains and the smaller the area becomes. It's the process of slowly working your way toward a correct *range* through incremental data collection.

For instance, I may guess that a company is producing ten widgets a day, while a coworker believes that the same company is only producing four widgets a day. An average of our estimates wouldn't be a bad idea. Then my supervisor might suppose that the company produces seven widgets a day. Then her supervisor chimes in and says that the figure is six. Slowly, we close in on a range that is somewhat supported by all the data points.

Now do this same process but with your opinions, stances, and perspectives.

You may feel that lemurs are the most ferocious animals alive (or insert a more inflammatory stance that I would rather not broach). A zoologist you know may assert that, while ferocious, they are third behind honey badgers and cornered cheetahs. A zookeeper you are acquainted with may knock the lemur down to fifth place, under hippos, beavers, eagles, cheetahs, and honey badgers. A veterinarian friend may place lemurs between the two at the fourth most ferocious, behind cheetahs, honey badgers, geese, and buffalo.

What have you gained from this exercise? Well, you know your initial opinion is probably wrong, and you also know what the correct range of answers is.

Officially, triangulation of information requires collecting and verifying information from at least two different sources. Optimally, there are many more. While the "peer review" form of triangulation is potentially the best, you can also obtain it by examining data or theories from other sources (in other words, research).

Subjecting your perspectives and ideas to peer review and triangulation increases your legitimacy and authenticity. It shows that you're confident enough to expose your solutions to outside scrutiny and that you have the humility to listen to other opinions and constructive criticism. And that adds a lot of weight and sureness to the decisions you make: it increases the likelihood that they're sound choices, ones that are well thought-out and tested through trials.

Through that process, you'll gain a sense of what the actual solution is and, related to the main thrust of the chapter, solve problems far easier and quicker.

MM #14: Find Your Own Flaws

Use to scrutinize yourself before others can.

Requesting the learned opinions of others can be illuminating, especially if they happen to confirm that your opinions and perspectives have been misguided.

But we can also do this for ourselves by invoking the mental model of searching for your own flaws. Treat your perspective or opinion as a hypothesis that must be tested and verified. Key to this is not being emotionally invested in the outcome, or defensive about being correct as opposed to seeking the honest truth.

Instead of approaching a perspective or opinion by seeking to prove it, flip it on its head and seek to prove it wrong (dogs aren't great; dogs are evil).

Instead of maximizing its supposed benefits, minimize them and maximize the shortcomings (dogs may be relatively loyal compared to cats, but they are high-maintenance and can be extremely costly and sometimes even violent).

Instead of imagining smooth sailing and a best-case scenario, paint an apocalyptic worst-case scenario (what if I get a violent dog that I can't properly train and he ruins everything in my home?).

Ask yourself this: if you wanted your perspective or opinion to fail, what is the easiest way for that to happen (if I don't give my dog enough attention or walks, he will go crazy and destroy things)?

Bleak, I know. But otherwise, you fall into the error of confirmation bias. Confirmation bias is rampant; it is when one only pursues and listens to information or evidence in favor of a certain belief that we wish to be true. In doing so, it causes one to disregard, rationalize, deny, or steer clear completely of evidence that disproves or challenges that belief. It's not necessarily driven by ego so much as it is by a desire for wanting to be correct.

Confirmation bias is the ultimate stance of seeing what you want to see and using that perception to prove a pre-chosen conclusion. In fact, it's where you start with a conclusion in mind and work backward to make it your reality despite evidence directly to the contrary.

The simplest example is when you have a particular stance that you want to support—for example, that dogs are loyal. So you type into Google "dogs are very loyal." Obviously, this is going to generate results about the loyalty of dogs, whereas if you type in (1) "are dogs loyal?" (2) "dogs loyalty," or (3) "dogs are not loyal," you would get a broader range of the literature on dogs and loyalty. This particular stance does not have any consequences, but confirmation bias can also turn life-threatening.

Finding your own flaws flows in the opposite (and correct) direction of starting with premises and then drawing conclusions only from what the evidence seems to honestly point toward. Most of us have veritable physical pain when we think about admitting our flaws, especially in front of others. But that's the ego talking, and the ego has zero interest in solving problems and thinking clearly. The ego will always have comforting yet detrimental motives.

The mental model of finding your own flaws applies in another important context: in relationships. This particularly arises when you have conflict with someone else. But again, what if you were to shift gears and proactively seek to find your own flaws in your arguments and stances instead of defending them to the death?

Instead, when you seek to find your own flaws in arguments, try to find what's known as the *third story*. The third story is what an objective bystander would say about the conflict. It would be ruthlessly objective and detached. You would probably not be pleased to hear it, and you would definitely not be found blameless or without fault.

This is an important realization in itself. Often we can get so wrapped up in intense emotion that we lose track of our goal and simply defend. That's easier for some people than it is for others, but conceding that you *could* be mistaken opens many more doors to understanding than entrenching yourself. Recognizing that your point of view may be imperfect is, in fact, usually the first part of solving a problem. It's a sign of strength and confidence, whereas dogged refusal to listen to another outlook is more frequently perceived as a sign of shakiness or weakness.

In that sense, it's good to handle your perspective as if there's at least *something* amiss about it—say, starting with 1%. There's almost no interpersonal issue where the answer is utterly black or white; you are not infallible. So what 1% are you probably wrong about in your side of the argument, even if you don't want to admit it?

If you can fully commit to 1% error/flaw, then it immediately opens you up to the other things you might be missing. Getting that third perspective is a great bridge to understanding the whole of a problem— because if the third story deviates drastically from your story and your opponent's story, then you probably aren't even thinking about the same problem to solve.

MM #15: Separate Correlation From Causation

Use to understand what truly needs to be addressed to solve a problem.

In efforts to understand why certain events happen, we must go looking for instigating factors. It's only logical that we try to find a previous event directly responsible for *causing* the event we're looking at. This is what we should spend our time trying to fix, but it turns out that we might be spending all of our time on the wrong issue. We're fooled into confusing correlation for causation. One of this mental model's shining examples follows.

Say you're looking at a graph that shows two data comparisons—one axis shows the total number of sunglasses sold over a period of time, and the other shows the total sales of ice cream. During the summer months, you note that sales of both items increase and that they tend to go down after summer is over.

Looking at this graph, you might come to the conclusion that sales of ice cream directly impact sales of sunglasses. People are buying more sunglasses because they're buying more ice cream—or the other way around. No matter the direction, it appears that one is causing the other.

Why might this be the case? Is it because there are stores that sell both ice cream *and* sunglasses? Is there something about buying a sundae or root beer float that triggers one to grab a pair of Ray-Bans immediately after? Do sunglasses press on a facial nerve that triggers thirst?

These theories sound ridiculous, don't they? That's because they are.

When you first read the example, you probably figured out that sales of ice cream and sunglasses increased due to the arrival of summer. Since there are more hot and sunny days in summer, people are more inclined to buy cold treats like ice cream and protective eyewear like sunglasses. People don't buy sunglasses as a direct result of ice cream purchases—they buy both when the summer heat hits them. Just because two things occur simultaneously doesn't mean there is a relationship *between* them.

Even though that's a pretty broad example, it reflects a logical error that lots of people make—sometimes about matters even *more* elementary and basic than ice cream and sunglasses. That error is believing that since two events have similar patterns or related behaviors that one must be causing the other to happen. This is the mistake of believing that *correlation implies causation*. In fact, they are entirely separate concepts.

Correlation is a statistical term. It shows that two individual elements or variables share similar traits or trends—"ice cream and sunglasses sales both *increased*." That's all there is to correlation: two things behave similarly in this way or that way. Correlation does *not* describe why or how the relationship between two items is the way it is; it doesn't give a reason. It just says, "These two things are generally doing the same thing at the same time."

Causation, on the other hand, is an effort to establish the reason things happen—also referred to as "cause and effect." The message of causation is: "This thing changed, which in turn *caused* this other thing to change." In our super-basic example, the thing that actually caused the increase in sunglasses revenue was the arrival of summer, which was also responsible for the increase in ice cream sales. There was a causal relationship between summer and sunglasses and summer and ice cream, but there's only a correlative relationship between sunglasses and ice cream.

To believe that the increase in ice cream sales *caused* the increase in sunglasses sales is a logical mistake. This is countered by the phrase *correlation doesn't imply causation*—just because two events are similar doesn't mean one is causing the other one to happen. There may be another underlying factor that's causing *both* things to happen.

This error in thinking usually happens when there's a lack of information at our disposal—or, perhaps more frequently, when we don't take the time to observe all the information we should. Jumping to conclusions is always a temptation when we feel under pressure to come up with a definitive answer. In order to avoid that fallacy, one should identify as many potential factors as one can: research, study trends, gather more data, and make reasonable, unhurried judgments.

In a lot of cases, correlations are nothing more than flukes or chance, yet we rapidly jump to causal thoughts. When evaluating cause and effect, the default mental model should always be to separate correlation from causation and not assume a causal relationship unless you can definitively say so.

There's one more wrinkle when it comes to discussing cause and effect. It's a bit more complex than we're led to believe as children, when we're taught that pushing on a toy truck will make it move.

As we gain more life experience, causal factors become a little more complex. There are more conditions, underlying motives, and elements that affect events. Sometimes it's hard to point to a singular cause, because it's hard to say that it acted alone or wasn't the product of multiple mini-causes.

This process involves looking past the immediate reason things happen (the *proximate* cause) and searching for certain greater, more fundamental basis that things happen (the *root* cause). The proximate cause is to the root cause as correlation is to plain causation. Solving for the former (proximate cause; correlation) won't rid you of your troubles.

For example, say somebody's driver's license gets suspended. Let's call him Hal. Traffic court has been waiting for Hal to respond to a series of speeding violations, but he's never complied. A warrant for Hal's arrest is issued; the police go over to his home, bust down his door, and throw him in jail for a long weekend.

At this point, we can ask the question, why is Hal in jail? Well, he's there because police were acting on an arrest warrant that said he needed to answer for multiple speeding violations. This is the *proximate* cause: the most recent, basic actions that led to Hal being thrown into the slammer.

But the proximate cause doesn't explain the deeper issues that have led to Hal's being in jail. You could say the arrest warrant was issued because Hal's a lead-foot who needs to lighten up on the accelerator pedal. So you could consider Hal's need for speed to be the *root* cause.

But is it?

One can keep going down a rabbit hole to find out *why* Hal is this way, and you could continue to consider each new level a *more* root cause. If he's going to change his ways, simply telling him to stop speeding so much might not be effective. What's causing him to speed? Maybe his parents never taught him restraint in certain situations; they just let him dart around the house and make a mess of things, and that recklessness followed him into adulthood. At this point, Hal has a *deeper* root cause—some have called this level arriving at the *ultimate* cause. Unless Hal deals with the emotional basis for his speeding habit, there's a great chance he'll re-offend. If he blows them off and just blames "the man," he hasn't learned anything.

This is the proximate/root cause portion of this mental model in a nutshell. It's a more critical and profound way of discovering the *real* answers and explanations for events. Quality thinking means going past the proximate cause—which is usually just a physical sequence of cues—and understanding the factors, thinking or emotional patterns, or environmental elements that set the groundwork for something happening.

It might help to imagine each set of actions as motivated by something psychological. One way of putting this discovery plan into action is the "five whys" method, which is simply asking "why" five times to establish a deeper root cause:

Why is Hal in jail? Because there was an arrest warrant out for him (proximate cause).

Why? Because he hadn't responded in court to his multiple speeding violations.

Why? Because he exceeded the speed limit nine times and got caught.

Why? Because he has a "need" or impulse to go super-fast on the highway.

Why? Because he never had a set of boundaries as a child and thought he could do whatever he wanted without consequences.

Differentiating between proximate and root causes makes one keep going in the discovery process—whereas, left to one's own instincts, they might just stop asking once they identify the immediate cause or even when they see a vague correlation. By going deeper you'll get a better understanding of why things happen and be better positioned to deal with problems.

MM #16: Storytell in Reverse

Use to determine causation more effectively.

Speaking of determining cause...

Now that you've learned a mental model to stop confusing correlation with causation, we delve deeper into causation than the five whys technique from the previous mental model. For those of us who are more artistically inclined, this is your moment to shine.

A *fishbone diagram* is a method that allows you to identify multiple potential causes for a problem or an effect. Being able to infer causes based on an observed effect is an integral aspect of deduction, especially when it comes to problem-solving. Fleshing out a list of all the possible causes of a problem simultaneously provides you with a blueprint of the specific factors you need to focus on to ultimately find viable solutions.

The fishbone diagram is so structured that those causes are placed in categories, so you get a more orderly perspective of the entire situation. It's a more organized way of working in reverse from effect to cause and is a frequently used tool for structuring brainstorming sessions. The end product is a visual display of all the factors—both from a micro and a macro perspective—

that play a role in leading to the effect or the problem.

To make a fishbone diagram, first write a problem statement or effect somewhere in the middle right portion of a whiteboard or any writing surface you've chosen. Draw a box around it, then a horizontal line across the page that ends in that problem box. That box will serve as the "head" of the fishbone.

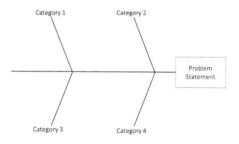

Next, draw the "bones" of the body by sketching widely spaced vertical lines that come out of the main horizontal line. Draw bones above and below the main line, slightly slanting away from the head of the fishbone. These bones will be labeled with the different categories of the causes you come up with. It's up to you to name the categories that apply to the problem you're working on.

Every time you come up with a possible cause for the problem, write it down as a connection to the particular "bone" it's categorized under. You can write the same cause under multiple categories, if applicable. Then, for each noted cause, continue asking what might've caused it and write it down as a connection to that cause—and so on until you can no longer think of a more primary cause. This will allow you to exercise your deductive reasoning skills until you arrive at the most fundamental root causes of the problem.

When you're done with the diagram, scrutinize the causes you've listed and consider the evidence regarding it. How much does the identified cause really contribute to creating the effect? Is its link with the problem well-established and significant enough to consider seriously? Get into the habit of thinking, "What would make this cause a true and significant factor in the problem at hand?"

For example, say you're a hotel manager trying to understand the causes of low customer satisfaction ratings for your hotel service. Write the problem in a box as the fishbone "head" and the categories of possible causes (in this case, the four P's of service industries) as the main "bones." Doing this, the initial stages of your fishbone diagram would look like so:

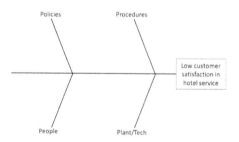

Then start filling in each category with possible causes. For example, you've identified that possible causes for the problem are (1) the slow resolution of customer complaints and (2) the hotel staff's inability to be sensitive to the customers' needs, thus leading the customer to being dissatisfied with the service.

Asking yourself why your staff may lack sensitivity to customer needs, you may consider that they work such long hours that they are reduced to providing just the bare minimum of service; they no longer have enough energy to pay more attention to customers' more specific needs. Given that, your fishbone diagram would now indicate the following:

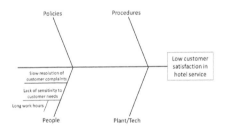

Continuing the process of asking yourself why the problem exists, you start identifying more possible causes and noting them under the given categories, leading your diagram to look something like this:

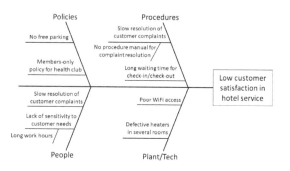

By systematically working backward from the problem to the causes, you get to identify specific aspects of your situation that you can then address accordingly. The fishbone diagram is a tool that effectively focuses your efforts to solve the problem at its roots—or, in this case, at its bones.

It's a great way to guide your thinking in the process of reverse storytelling, as it allows you to concretely trace how the problem is linked back to specific causative factors.

Try observing a scene, a person, or any other thing and observing ten details about it. Then, for each of those details, write down five possible causes that may have led that particular detail to be the way it is. Try to vary the potential causes you list down, ranging from the plainly realistic to the downright bizarre. This will train your ability to create a story around every detail and consider what preceded it, thus exercising your skills in reverse storytelling.

MM #17: SCAMPER It

Use to methodically and creatively solve problems with force-fitting.

Lists of mental models can sometimes start to feel like checklists.

That's a feature, not a bug. In other words, that is their intended function, because otherwise, as a human, you have the tendency to forget things or let things slip through the cracks. To that end, with this mental model, we're really going to institute the checklist feeling because SCAMPER is all about a methodical approach to solving problems and finding solutions.

Pioneered by Bob Eberle to spark creativity during brainstorming sessions, the SCAMPER method stands for seven techniques that help direct thinking toward novel ideas and solutions: (S) substitute, (C) combine, (A) adapt, (M) minimize/magnify, (P) put to another use, (E) eliminate, and (R) reverse. Collectively, these techniques are based on the idea that you can come up with something new by simply modifying the old things already present around you.

Think of this mental model as akin to opening a faucet that introduces water to seven pipes, and each of those pipes channels to a unique pot of earth. Each pot has the potential to bring forth a new growth once the seeds in it are watered. Note that the SCAMPER method doesn't require that you move in a sequential flow of steps. You can use it in any order or sequence and jump among the different techniques.

Furthermore, it encourages the principle of *force-fitting,* a candidate for a mental model in itself. This means that in order to come up with fresh solutions, you should be willing to integrate ideas, objects, or elements—no matter how dissimilar, unrelated, or apparently illogical they seem to be. This is a major element of SCAMPER because we are too often held back by our preconceptions and assumptions of what *cannot* be.

Substitute. This technique refers to replacing certain parts in the product, process, or service with another to solve a problem. To carry out this technique, first consider the situation or problem in light of having many elements—multiple materials, several steps in the process, different times or places at which the process can occur, various markets for the product or service, and the like. Then consider that each and every one of these elements may be replaced with an alternative.

Some questions that might help you get into this flow of thinking include the following: "Could a more cost-effective material replace the current one we're using without sacrificing product quality?" "What part of the process can be switched into a simpler alternative?" "In what other places can we offer our services?"

Let's say you're into the production of craft pieces that use a particular kind of glue as adhesive. However, you find that the glue you use easily dries out and clumps up even when stored properly, leading to wastage and more production costs. To solve this problem, consider brainstorming whether you might use a different adhesive to replace what you're currently using. Another example might be substituting local materials for imported ones, not only reducing costs on your end but also helping the local community in the process.

Combine. This technique suggests considering whether two products, ideas, or steps of a procedure may be combined to produce a single output or process that's better in some way. Two existing products could create something new if put together. Two old ideas could merge into a fresh, groundbreaking one if fused in the right way. Two stages of a process may be melded into one to create a more streamlined, efficient procedure.

Questions that can facilitate a line of thinking utilizing the combined technique include the following: "Can we put two or more elements together?" "Can we carry out two processes at the same time?" "Can we join forces with another company to improve our market strength?"

For instance, the combination of the spoon and fork has led to the innovation of the spork, a utensil now often packed within ready-to-eat noodle cups because of its cost-saving and convenient design. It solves the problem of having to manufacture two different utensils and effectively halves the cost of production.

Adapt. This technique intends to adjust something in order to enhance it. It solves problems by improving on how things are typically done, with adjustments ranging from something small to something radical. It challenges you to think of ways that you can adjust what's already existing—be it a product, a process, or a manner of doing things—such that it solves a current problem and is better tailored to your needs.

Noticing that you have less energy than usual, for instance, you may think of solving the problem by making adjustments to your food choices, such as cutting back on empty calories and processed food. In the business world, this technique is also often utilized by brainstorming groups looking to enhance their product, service, or production process.

Some questions considered under this rubric include the following: "How can we regulate the existing process to save us more time?" "How can we tweak the existing product to sell better?" "How can we adjust the existing process to be more cost-effective?"

An example of an adaptation for a product is the development of mobile phone cases that have been imbued with shock absorbers or shockproof material. This clever tweak has obviously been developed in response to the common problem of accidentally dropping and consequently damaging fragile phone parts. In a similar vein, waterproofing mobile phone cases, wristwatches, and the like is another instance of adapting a product in order to improve it.

Magnify or minimize. This technique involves either increasing or decreasing an element to trigger new ideas and solutions. Magnifying pertains to increasing something, such as by exaggerating a problem, putting more emphasis on an idea, making a product bigger or stronger, or doing a process more frequently.

On the other hand, minimizing entails decreasing something, such as by toning down a problem, deemphasizing an idea, reducing the size of a product, or carrying out a process less frequently. Thinking through certain elements in terms of either magnifying or minimizing them is bound to give you fresh insights as to the most and least significant parts of your problem, thus guiding you toward effective solutions.

Discussion questions that apply the magnify technique include the following: "How can you exaggerate or overstate the problem?" "What would be the outcome if you emphasized this feature?" "Will doing the process more frequently make a difference?" As for minimizing, challenge yourself to ponder the following: "How will playing down this feature change the outcome?" "How can we condense this product?" "Will doing this step less frequently lead to better efficiency?"

Say that you've been assigned to transfer to a smaller office. You now have the problem of fitting your things into a more confined space. Using the magnify and minimize technique to resolve your dilemma, you can ask yourself questions as to which office components you would want to place more or less emphasis on. Are you going to place more emphasis on having space for receiving and meeting with clients or for tech equipment or maybe for file storage?

Mulling over which aspect to magnify will help you pick out and arrange things in your new office in a way that best reflects your needs and values. As for using the minimize technique, consider which of your office stuff may be condensed together to fit a smaller floor area. For example, while previously you may have had separate tables for your computer and your printer, you may think of using a compact computer desk with a printer shelf instead.

Put to another use. This technique aims to figure out how an existing product or process may be used for a purpose other than what it's currently being used for. It stimulates a discussion on the myriad of other ways you might find a use for anything from raw materials to finished products to discarded waste. It's basically about finding a new purpose for old things.

Some questions that can facilitate this line of thinking include the following: "How else can this product be used?" "Can another part of the company use this material?"

"Can we find a use for the bits we throw out?"

Consider how this would apply for stuff lying around in your own home. For instance, how would you address the problem of old newspapers just piling up in a corner? Using them to clean your window panes is a common solution, but how about finding other fresh ways to use them? By challenging yourself to think of more unconventional uses, you will magnify the way those old newspapers benefit you, from serving as trusty deodorizers for shoes to being raw materials for fun papier-mâché crafts.

Eliminate. This technique refers to identifying the unnecessary elements of a project or process so that they can be eliminated and thus provide for an improved outcome. It considers how a procedure may be streamlined by dropping redundant steps or how the same output may be produced despite cutting resources. Whatever resource is freed up may then be used to enhance creativity and innovation.

Questions that make up this rubric include the following: "Is there any step we can remove without affecting the outcome?" "How would we carry out the same activity if we had half the resources?" "What would happen if we eliminated this part?"

One of the most useful applications of this technique is in the area of addressing financial problems in daily life. For example, you find that you're earning enough for your daily expenses but never get to put money aside for emergencies. Barring the option of gaining more income, the only thing left to do is to subtract expenses so you can save for an emergency fund.

Using the eliminate technique, identify expenses you can cut—maybe pass up on buying that shiny new bag you don't really need or opt for cheaper home-cooked meals instead of dining out. The money freed up from eliminating unnecessary expenses can then be your savings for use come rainy days.

Reverse. This technique suggests switching up the order of the process steps in order to find solutions and maximize innovative potentials. Also known as the rearrange technique, this line of thinking encourages interchanging elements or considering the process backward in order to stimulate a fresh take on the situation.

Some questions that apply the reverse technique include the following: "How would reversing the process change the outcome?" "What would happen if we did the procedure backward?" "Can we interchange one step with another?"

Say you're having trouble fulfilling your personal promise to exercise more. You've had it written in your schedule to spend 30 minutes exercising at the end of the day. But when it comes time for it, you always seem to have other more urgent things to attend to or are too tired for it. Thus, you never get around to doing it consistently. To solve this problem, you may consider applying the reverse technique.

Check whether you may interchange your exercise time slot with another part of your day, such as making time for it first thing in the morning instead. By reversing the time you set for exercising, you may just find it easier to stick to the routine, as in the morning you're not yet drained or too beset by the day's activities.

The SCAMPER method is one of the easiest yet most effective strategies for finding solutions to problems and sparking creative thinking. Because a process is explored from seven different perspectives—substitute, combine, adapt, modify, put to another use, eliminate, and reverse—no stone is left unturned, and even unconventional solutions can be uncovered. Where you had one or two ways of looking at a problem, you now have seven additional approaches to apply.

MM #18: Get Back to First Principles

Use to break preconceptions and find your own solution.

Finally, famed South African entrepreneur Elon Musk asks the simple question to help us solve problems: *how can we be sure that we aren't attempting to solve a problem based on imperfect or incomplete information?*

Welcome to the mental model of *first principles thinking*, which is stripping everything about a problem away until you only have the basic components—because only then are you free to really address the problem itself.

Much of the thinking and analysis we do rests on the backs of other people's accomplishments, discoveries, and assumptions. We'll see how someone else does something—builds a bicycle, makes a cake, writes a song, opens a small business—and, more or less, copy what they did and just add a few things to improve it. We don't think much about them, and we follow suit for various reasons, one of which is "it's just the way it's always been done." Why do we need to reinvent the wheel?

It may not be innovative or original, but following a proven guideline works. Or does it?

This is known as *analogy reasoning*, and it *works*, but it is prone to errors and mistakes because you follow a path like gospel while underlying assumptions aren't questioned. Imagine if you were told that a cake has a certain amount of flour and eggs, and you simply emulated the recipe without questioning as if it were true. This recipe may have been handed down for generations, but perhaps it was simply codified because one grandmother down the line only had so much flour and eggs available to make the cake. Perhaps this actually creates a rather gross-tasting cake, and if you deviated, you would improve the flavor and moistness tenfold.

The point is that what we think we know about a problem or scenario is often based on a set of assumptions. Assumptions aren't always correct. We assume that flour and eggs in a specific ratio create the best-tasting cake, but is it true? You just might be the blind following the blind. (Sorry to all the grandmothers.)

First principles thinking is the practice of obliterating this tendency to *follow* and breaking assumptions down until only basic factors remain. Reasoning by first principles removes the impurity of assumptions and conventions.

This method strips away the opinions and interpretations of other people and gets you to the essential elements that exist. From there, you can then build back up to a solution, often with an entirely new approach based on truths that are unimpeachable and indisputable—because you are not resting on any assumptions anymore.

Thus, breaking grandma's cake down to first principles would be to first examine what is actually needed to bake a cake and in what proportions. Only then could you start to recreate the cake to be tastier, and you might find that different proportions and ingredients are needed. It sounds like an easy solution, but sometimes it just doesn't occur to us that not everything is set in stone.

Musk espouses first principle thinking in everything he does and fervently denies being told "that is impossible." Sure, it might be impossible according to the assumptions currently in place, but not *his*.

When Musk sought to create SpaceX, a privatized space company, he quickly ran into the reason that all other privatized similar efforts had failed: the massive cost of rockets. Being that the business of SpaceX would be sending rockets into space, this was quite a roadblock.

But his price estimates rested on the assumption that he would have to buy rockets from other companies. He applied first principles thinking and broke down the real costs of getting into outer space through any means, and he quickly found that the price tag of the rocket wasn't what it seemed.

Instead of buying a *finished* rocket for up to $65 million USD, Musk decided to *insource* the process, purchase the raw materials, and build the rockets himself. Within a few years, SpaceX had cut the price of launching a rocket to a fraction—by some reports 10% of his earlier estimates.

Musk used first principles thinking to break the situation down to the fundamentals and simply asked what was needed to get into outer space. A rocket—that answer didn't change. But the rocket didn't have to come from Boeing or Lockheed or any of the other established aerospace manufacturing companies. By starting from his goal and then identifying the inherent assumptions he wanted to break free of, he was able to create a more efficient solution. You start by asking, "What are we 100% sure is true and proven? Okay, let's disregard everything besides that."

He used his mental model once again when he wanted to solve the problem of fast and efficient transportation between Los Angeles and San Francisco.

The current assumptions around such a solution are numerous. The obvious frontrunner would be a high-speed rail system similar to Korea and Japan's subway systems. However, it's an assumption that his new method of transportation would need to resemble any existing systems. What about reinventing the wheel?

The fundamentals of his problem were that he wanted a safer, faster, and cheaper method—it could conform to existing transportation systems, but it didn't need to. With those requirements, what kind of new system could be created? That's when the Hyperloop was born, and if you've seen pictures of it, it resembles an underground roller coaster more than a rail system. But that doesn't matter if the problem is solved, does it?

To find first principles, Musk goes through a short three-step process to blow past assumptions. For our purposes, let's suppose our problem is to recreate grandma's cake with a lack of the ingredients in the recipe.

1. Identify and define current assumptions. These are things that appear to be givens or unable to change. Grandma's

cake requires a certain mixture of flour and eggs. Or does it?

2. Break down the problem into its first principles. Something edible resembling a cake must be presented. A cake typically requires X number of eggs and Y grams of flour. It needs heat and a container.

3. Create new solutions from scratch. Grandma's cake is unable to be created with the current ingredients we have, but we can find adequate substitutes for everything missing. What substitutions can be made in the recipe? Does it even have to be flour or eggs at all?

You can use this model of thought for just about anything—building a business, learning history or the arts, even analyzing an emotional or personal issue. For example, your problem is that you don't seem to have enough time in your schedule to exercise sufficiently to lose weight.

Assumptions: Weight loss depends on exercise, you don't have enough time, you need to lose that much weight, your schedule is too busy.

First principles: Weight loss depends mostly on diet, you can make time if you stop watching so much television, your schedule still allows a few 20-minute breaks throughout the day, and you don't actually need to lose *that* much weight.

New method: A combination of short, quick workouts and eating healthier by preparing all of your week's meals on Sunday.

Just by going through the investigative process that first principles thinking espouses, one can see more clearly all the elements, individual components, and parts of a situation. First principles thinking isn't easy; if it were, then everyone would do it.

Takeaways:

- Most of the ways we solve problems amount to running into the same wall and hoping that it will eventually crumble. Obviously, this is not optimal for us or the wall. Better problem-solving can certainly stem from mental models because they can provide a formula for us to follow. After all, that's all things like the quadratic equation or π are—mental models to help us solve problems.

- Mental Model #13: Peer Review Your Perspectives. Many of the ways we fail at solving problems are related to our inability to look at other perspectives. In fact, we should be continually checking our perspectives through triangulation against those of others. Thinking and solving in a vacuum will never work because if you didn't experience it firsthand, it won't make sense to you.

- Mental Model #14: Find Your Own Flaws. This mental model is about resisting the comforting allure of confirmation bias and attempting to scrutinize yourself before others ever get the chance. Assume that you are wrong; this especially applies to interpersonal relationships. If you assume that you are at least 1% responsible for conflict, then your illusion of superiority and infallibility is broken, an important factor in social interaction.

- Mental Model #15: Separate Correlation From Causation. They are entirely different things. Forcing a relationship where none exists will cause you to chase the wrong issue. In addition, you must separate proximate cause from root cause—root cause is what we always want, and it can be reached through a series of questions.

- Mental Model #16 Storytell in Reverse. When it comes to causation, sometimes we just need to get better at thinking in a certain manner. You have a visual aid in a fishbone diagram, which goes on to document causes of causes and so on. This is storytelling in reverse because you start with a conclusion and you work backward through sometimes ambiguous means.

- Mental Model #17: SCAMPER It. The SCAMPER method stands for seven techniques that help direct thinking toward novel ideas and solutions: (S) substitute, (C) combine, (A) adapt, (M) minimize/magnify, (P) put to another use, (E) eliminate, and (R) reverse.

- Mental Model #18: Get Back to First Principles. When we try to solve problems, oftentimes we attempt to follow methods or a specific path just because they are the conventional means. But are they the best? First principles thinking strips away assumptions and leaves you with only a set of facts and a desired outcome. From there, you can forge your own solution.

Chapter 4. Anti-Mental Models: How Avoidance Breeds Success

We've examined some mental models for how to handle certain situations, improve our reasoning, solve problems, and attack some of the thornier issues in life head-on. Some of them are a set of guidelines on how to think, and others end up prescribing a specific sequence of actions.

These are helpful, but they all have one thing in common: they are all aiming toward some sort of end goal. The mental model sets a goal to strive for, whether it is about seeing regressions to the mean, focusing on important tasks as opposed to urgent tasks, or triangulating your perspectives and opinions into improvement. The closer you get to what you strive toward, the closer you get to achievement.

There's nothing wrong with this, and we are naturally predisposed to it as it's the sort of template we are raised on. If you want to do well in school, you shoot for high marks and showing all your work. If you want to be the fastest competitive swimmer, you strive for the fastest times and best technique. Whatever the goal, your intention should be to move closer to it.

But this doesn't always produce the best results, and furthermore, it doesn't always represent where our priorities should lie.

Sometimes (actually, you'll find this to be frequent and widespread), it's both easier and more representative of your true priorities to aim *away* from a certain *negative* threshold/milestone than it is to aim toward a certain *positive* threshold/milestone.

As a quick illustration, suppose you want to learn to swim better. You could keep in mind each tip on how to improve your technique (long strokes). But you could also think about the things that a terrible swimmer does and avoid those at all costs (avoid short strokes). You would get a similar end result, and possibly a better one because you would focus on removing your weak points.

We can refer to these as *anti-mental models,* as they still provide a blueprint of guidance, but they are about moving away from something rather than toward it. Just as we have mental models for getting what we want out of life, we also have ways of thinking that can help us avoid the things we *don't* want. It can take just as much human resolve and strategy to break away from things as it does to get what we want. In both cases you're trying to be the best human being you can be.

For example, what if you want to be a better friend? Instead of creating a list of excellent friend attributes, you could start by creating a list of things you'd hate people to do to you and avoid those. This may actually yield even better results.

Do you want to be more productive? Instead of asking yourself how to be more productive, ask yourself what sabotages your productivity and make it your goal to avoid those.

Sometimes, a simple shift in perspective is what we need to be more effective. What resonates with one person may not resonate with the next, even though they have extremely similar sentiments. Either way, it's all about what moves you into consistent action.

The concept of anti-mental models also points our attention to something that is usually overlooked: dealing with negatives.

If your swimming technique is 99% amazing, that 1% will still keep you back. Achieving a host of positive goals usually doesn't matter if a glaring negative exists. Often, what matters in life is the lack of any negatives rather than the presence of positives. Ask anyone if they care that they have the most expensive and luxurious shoes when the shoes pinch their toes to the point of bleeding with every step. Our weakest links are usually what hold us back or keep us unfulfilled, and with anti-mental models, you are taking care of them up front.

Consider that money doesn't buy you happiness, yet removing anxiety surrounding security, housing, food, providing, and hunger will generally make people impervious to misery. Aiming to remove negatives sets a minimum floor of fulfillment and achievement; usually we are aiming to blast through the roof, and this isn't what will actually make an impact on us.

This chapter looks at some anti-mental models that will provide you with clarity on how avoidance of negatives can breed just as much success as directly pursuing goals.

MM #19: Avoid Direct Goals

Use to find clarity in how to reach your overarching destination.

We'll pick up right where we began—with how to create anti-mental models where you focus on avoiding something. These are just as effective at driving you toward a goal. We start with a very clear one: avoid *direct* goals. Like before, to achieve the outcome we want, we want to avoid working toward something and instead work to avoid a negative. Instead of direct goals, we want *inverse goals*, also known as *anti-goals*.

Carl Jacobi, a German mathematician, was known for utilizing such an approach to solve difficult math problems. Following a strategy of *man muss immer umkehren*, or "invert, always invert," Jacobi would write down math problems in inverse form and find that it was easier for him to arrive at the solution that way: by first finding what *wasn't* possible.

Transferring this inverse way of thinking to life at large, Charlie Munger challenges the youth to ponder on the inverse of success instead of simply focusing on how to achieve success.

He poses the question, "What do you want to avoid?" and offers a likely response: sloth and unreliability. These qualities are roadblocks to success, and you get to shine a spotlight on them precisely by asking why people fail instead of why they succeed. By inverting the question of success, you get to discover drivers of failure and are thus able to avoid such behaviors in order to improve. In other words, if you work hard to avoid sloth and unreliability, success should be yours.

So instead of asking what you need to do to be a better manager, try considering what a terrible manager would do. Avoid those actions. If your business model centers on innovation, ask "How could we *limit* this company's innovative potentials?" Do the opposite. If you're looking to improve your productivity, ask "What are the things I do to distract myself?" Generally, instead of asking "How do I solve this problem," ask "How would I *cause* this problem?" Then do something else.

Inversion helps you uncover your hidden beliefs and allows you to avoid what you ultimately don't want. You can find sudden clarity when you realize that success might truly only depend on the *absence* of something.

It's much easier to avoid what you don't want than to get what you do want. The easiest way to use anti-goals or inverse goals just takes two steps. It applies neatly to nearly anything you wish to achieve.

1. Define failure or causes of unhappiness.

2. Create methods to avoid those things at all costs.

For instance, do you want to improve the quality of your days?

1. Define failure or causes of unhappiness. For instance, what defines a poor-quality day? Four factors: poor sleep, bad traffic, poor diet, and an annoying dog.

2. Create methods to avoid those things at all costs. How can you address each of these contributors to unhappy days? Buy a new bed or find a new sleep ritual. Find ways to make your commute more enjoyable or minimal or shift your work hours around so you can avoid it completely. Pack your lunches beforehand or learn how to cook healthier. Buy the dog some more chew toys, hire a dog walking service, or get him a buddy.

When we reduce this anti-mental model down even further, the most powerful and simple version is to *just avoid stupidity*. We typically seek to act smart and clever, and again, this is how we are taught to think from childhood.

It's not wrong, but it does leave room for some improvement. Trying to do smart things can be perilous and ambiguous. It's an open-ended task. But avoiding stupidity, well, that's pretty apparent when you see it. Munger, on the topic of stupidity:

It is remarkable how much long-term advantage people like us have gotten by trying to be consistently not stupid, instead of trying to be very intelligent. There must be some wisdom in the folk saying, "It's the strong swimmers who drown."

I sought good judgment mostly by collecting instances of bad judgment, then pondering ways to avoid such outcomes.

A lot of success in life and business comes from knowing what you want to avoid: early death, a bad marriage, etc... Just avoid things like racing trains to the crossing, doing cocaine, etc. Develop good mental habits... Avoid evil, particularly if they're attractive members of the opposite sex.

We want to see what has caused businesses to go bad... I've often felt there might be more to be gained by studying business failures than business successes. In my business, we try to study where people go astray, and why things don't work.

Keep it simple. Think of anti-mental models as harnessing one of humanity's most obvious impulses: avoiding pain and discomfort. It's why we have phobias and anxieties and can't help but eat junk food. This is what has been programmed into us and has kept us alive for eons. Use it for good this time!

MM #20: Avoid Thinking Like an Expert

Use to strategically be able to see both the forest (big picture) and the trees (finer details).

Most of us are experts at *something*, whether it's a big, broad subject like science or arts or something more specific like cooking, exercise, or embroidery. We feel very comfortable in our knowledge in these areas, and we should. Having in-depth understanding and fluency in a field is a pillar of self-confidence. This seems like a good thing.

You can never have too much knowledge about a given field. In fact, the more you learn, it's likely that the less you feel that you know.

But is it possible that our confidence in understanding and knowledge in the "big picture" can result in our occasionally neglecting the small details? And can our expertise in a certain domain make us miss simple solutions outside our field of understanding?

A common saying tells us to avoid "missing the forest for the trees." The meaning is that when you focus on the small details (trees), you tend to either lose focus or stop paying attention to the big picture (forest). This would be when you become far too invested in playing a video game (tree) when the original point of the video game was to spend time with your significant other and improve the relationship (forest).

And of course, the inverse also applies; you can also "miss the trees for the forest," where you focus on the big picture to the detriment of glossing over smaller details. When we have expertise in a field, we tend to fall into this permutation because we take a look at something and it instantly generates a host of reactions and thoughts. If you were an expert musician and you looked at a piece of music, you aren't necessarily going to be concerned with the placement of every note, the notations, or an errant sharp or flat. You'll think about the overall melody, direction, feeling, phrasing, dynamics, and composition— thinking about the *forest* is an expert thought.

And it was in this exact context that this anti-mental model was conceived: *avoid thinking like an expert (occasionally), because experts don't always think about the little details. Don't* think like an expert. This is due to a psychological phenomenon called a *Goldovsky error*, and it is a type of small error that is easily spotted only by people who *lack* experience in a field. The more your expertise grows, the harder it becomes to spot those small errors. Experts skim and make assumptions about the basics because that's how their world works; they don't act as a spell-check.

Piano teacher Boris Goldovsky discovered a misprint in the sheet music of a Johannes Brahms piece that had been widely reproduced. More accurately, *he* didn't discover it until a neophyte pupil of his played the written note, which was wrong, time after time and he was confused by the dissonant sound.

Goldovsky wondered why no one, from composers to publishers, pianists, and other musicians, had noticed the error. It seemed impossible to escape notice. He eventually conducted studies that showed that skilled musicians *always* missed the error (even when they knew there was an error somewhere in the piece) because they made assumptions about the note that was supposed to be there and how the note fit into the overall piece. In the end, the only person to discover it on their own was that one novice student.

Thinking like an expert is by no means a bad practice, as it's what gives rise to new connections, advancements in thought, and overall learning. But for our purposes, it does create some rather large pitfalls that lead us to missing the trees for the forest: skimming, glossing over details, assumptions, unproven connections, and thinking about what something should or can be versus what it currently is.

In 1995 a movie called *Braveheart* was released to much acclaim—it eventually won the Oscar for Best Picture. *Braveheart* is about the Scottish fighter William Wallace, who led a fight against the Scottish king in the 13th and 14th centuries. For all of *Braveheart*'s technical brilliance, it contains one of the more notable gaffes in film history.

In one clip we see a massive army advancing toward a battle in slow motion, riding horses, hoisting weapons, generally looking ready to bust some skulls. But down in the lower-left corner of the screen there's a white automobile. If you've seen *Braveheart* you probably missed this car, because the shot it's in takes all of one second. You can verify this claim on YouTube.

Undoubtedly, everyone who made *Braveheart*—the director, the cinematographer, the script supervisor, pretty much everybody on the set—spent months on the project and probably had it uppermost in their minds the entire time. They had to get the sets and the costumes right, they had to choreograph the battle scenes so they looked exciting, they had to concentrate on the historical narrative, and so forth. More importantly, they were certainly experts. But somehow, everybody connected with *Braveheart* missed the fact that there was an SUV in the middle of a medieval battle.

This is another example of what we're talking about: being so wrapped up and focused on the big picture that a minor but significant detail is completely overlooked.

To avoid thinking like an expert, separate your thinking into two modes: expert and novice. As you've learned, they tend to focus on completely different aspects of a given topic. To think like an expert, well, do what you would usually do. Thinking like a novice requires you to humble yourself and not skip steps.

If an experienced chef looks at a recipe, they usually don't need to read the instructions. All they need is the list of ingredients; combined with their knowledge of how different kinds of dishes are prepared, they'll instantly know what needs to be done. A novice would need to go through all the steps individually and slowly. And in that slow process, they would pick out details and even potential mistakes that the experts would miss otherwise because of their assumptive nature.

Yes, harping on every small detail, particularly when you're confident about your field of expertise, can be annoying, trying, and frustrating. But it's also dramatically effective in cutting down on mistakes and even major catastrophes.

MM #21: Avoid Your Non-Genius Zones

Use to decide what you must focus your resources and time on.

The typical mental model here would be to stay in your zone of genius. Thus, this anti-mental model is about avoiding things that lie outside that zone of genius.

It's good to be ambitious and expand your skills and learn as many things as possible. We can all do this to an extent. We will never grow if we don't leave our comfort zone and try new things. But the point here isn't about growth; it's about actual performance. A select few of us seem to have otherworldly talents in just about everything we pursue, but for our purposes, let's assume we don't fall into that category.

Despite our ability to learn new skills and knowledge, there will always be a hierarchy—things that we can naturally excel at, whether it's because of time and experience or natural talent, and things that will always be difficult for us.

Take Mike.

He's one of the most talented and versatile musicians you could ever hope to come across. He's an exceptional pianist who can read sheet music by sight (an increasingly rare skill to have these days) and can figure out songs by ear. He parlayed some of this talent into musical theater, where he discovered he was a surprisingly good actor and a shockingly soulful singer. Mike could do almost everything to a high degree of competence in the musical theater world.

But Mike could not dance. He had great rhythm, great timing, and a great sense of tempo. He could execute all of it flawlessly when he played or sang. But he just couldn't put it together and *dance* to save his life. This didn't stop him from auditioning for parts that required a fair amount of dancing. These auditions became a great source of amusement for others who were watching and a painful source of embarrassment for Mike.

He shot himself in the foot, because while he was being offered a multitude of parts that were light on dancing and heavy on all of his other talents, he stubbornly insisted on being the classic "triple threat" of dancing, singing, and acting. Sooner rather than later, casting producers realized he wouldn't accept their offers, and the offers stopped coming.

Mike was operating outside of his zone of genius. He lacked the self-awareness to know what his strength and weaknesses were and capitalize on them. He insisted on acting as if he would have similar efficacy and performance in all three areas (dancing, singing, acting) because they were all related. He was wrong. Don't be like Mike.

It's great to be proficient at a lot of things. But it's also great—and arguably more human—to *know your limitations,* and that's really what this anti-mental model is about. There are certain things you will never develop great acumen or ability in. Recognizing those limitations is a part of developing who you are as a person. It's not an acknowledgment that you've failed at life, just that you will fail at this one particular thing. So accept it, avoid it, and stay where you are naturally talented. It's where you are most effective and even feel the best.

Don't set yourself up for failure by operating outside of your zone of genius. Set yourself up for consistent, reliable success by operating inside your zone of genius. Figure out your strategic advantages and exploit them to the max. Don't delude yourself by showcasing your weaknesses; rather, plan around them.

Just to reiterate, feel free to develop that range of abilities as much as you see fit. But recognize that you will always have a calling card or a set of skills that you are naturally better at. Don't feel ashamed or embarrassed about having restrictions— instead, feel confident about what you can do.

Here's what Charlie Munger (yes, again) had to say on the topic:

We'd rather deal with what we understand. Why should we want to play a competitive game in a field where we have no advantages—maybe a disadvantage—instead of playing in a field where we have a clear advantage? Each of you will have to figure out where your talent lies. And you'll have to use your advantages. But if you try to succeed in what you're worst at, you're going to have a very lousy career. I can almost guarantee it. To do otherwise, you'd have to buy a winning lottery ticket or get very lucky somewhere else.

That Munger guy is *good*.

MM #22: Avoid To-Do Lists

Use to direct your attention only to what matters at the moment.

This mental model delves into a different realm: productivity.

Sometimes when we're struggling to get started, it's because we can't choose what to fixate on. Too many things have the potential to command our focus, and sometimes we can't differentiate between what we should avoid and what actually deserves our attention.

Everyone knows the value of the to-do list, but this isn't as helpful as you might think because everyone inherently *kind of* knows what they should be doing and when they need to do it by. The act of writing it down just helps remind them. This makes them more likely to do what they know they should be doing—more than if they didn't have such a list.

The underrated problem most of us deal with is that we can't prioritize, and thus we don't know what we should and *shouldn't* be doing. Each day, we're faced with choosing tasks that will create the biggest impact for us, and there are many hidden obstacles. Thus, along with your to-do list, it's equally important to make a *don't-do list*.

The contents of a don't-do list might be surprising. We all know the obvious evils to avoid when trying to boost productivity: social media, goofing around on the Internet, watching *The Bachelorette* while trying to work, or learning to play the flute while reading. These are tasks with clearly zero benefit toward productivity.

You need to fill your don't-do list with tasks that will sneakily steal your time and undermine your goals. These are tasks that are insignificant or a poor use of your time, tasks that don't help your bottom line, and tasks that have a serious case of diminishing returns the more you work on them. They are *useless*, but it can be difficult to distinguish between real tasks and useless tasks, and it will require some hard thought on your part.

Perhaps like with the other anti-mental models, we will be able to narrow down our

192

priorities just by eliminating what doesn't belong. This works well when paired with the Eisenhower Matrix from an earlier chapter.

There are a few categories of tasks that belong on the don't-do list.

First, include tasks may be priorities, but you can't do anything about them at present because of external circumstances. These are tasks that are important in one or many ways but are waiting for feedback from others or for underlying tasks to be completed first. Put these on your don't-do list because there is literally nothing you can do about them, so they are just clogging up your mental bandwidth.

They'll still be there when you hear back from those other people. Just note that you are waiting to hear back from someone else and the date on which you need to follow-up if you haven't heard back. Then push these out of your mind, because they're on someone else's to-do list, not yours.

You can also temporarily push things off your plate by clarifying and asking questions of other people. This puts the ball in their court to act, and you can take that time to catch up on other matters.

Second, include tasks that don't add value as far as your priorities are concerned.

There are many small items that don't add to your bottom line, and often, these are trivial things—busywork. Can you delegate these, assign them to someone else, or even outsource them? Do they really require your time? In other words, are they *worth* your time? And will anyone but you notice the difference if you delegate the task to someone else? By taking on the task yourself, are you getting stuck in the weeds of perfectionism? These tasks are just wasted motion for the sake of motion and don't really matter in the big picture.

You should spend your time on big tasks that move entire projects forward and not myopic, trivial tasks.

Third, include tasks that are current and ongoing but will not benefit from additional work or attention paid to them. These tasks suffer from diminishing returns.

These tasks are just a waste of energy because while they can still stand to improve (and is there anything that can't?), the amount of likely improvement will either not make a difference in the overall outcome, or will take a disproportionate amount of time and effort without making a significant dent.

For all intents and purposes, these tasks should be considered *done*. Don't waste your time on them, and don't fall into the trap of considering them a priority. Once you finish everything else on your plate, you can then evaluate how much time you want to devote to polishing something.

If the task is at 90% of the quality you need it to be, it's time to look around at what else needs your attention to bring it from 0% to 90%. In other words, it's far more helpful to have three tasks completed at 80% quality versus one task at 100% quality.

Fourth and finally, urgent tasks! Refer to MM #1.

When you consciously avoid the items on your don't-do list, you keep yourself focused and streamlined. You don't waste energy or time, and your daily output will increase dramatically.

It would be like reading a menu with food items that are unavailable. It's pointless. By preventing your energy level from being dissipated by those things that suck up your time and attention, a don't-do list enables you to take care of the important stuff first.

The fewer things that tug on your mind, the better—the kind of stress and anxiety they create only hampers or kills productivity. A don't-do list will free your mind of the burden of having too many things in the air because it eliminates most of those things. You can focus on the balls that are still in flight and steadily knock each one out.

MM #23: Avoid the Path of Least Resistance

Use to exercise more self-discipline and willpower.

Too often, we get sucked into the path of least resistance. We might even perform mental gymnastics to convince ourselves that this path is the one we should be walking. In either case, we are stuck walking down a path that leads away from our best interests. We're a lazy species that doesn't want to do anymore than what is necessary at the present moment. Predictably, this can work against us.

This mental model is about avoiding what appears too simple, too easy, and too good to be true—because it probably is, and you're missing out on the path you should be taking instead. There is an *easy* path and a *right* path—often you'll find yourself on the right path if you just avoid the path of least resistance. Seek the resistance; seek the hardship, and rest assured that you are on the correct path. Chances are avoiding struggle will just lead you away from what you want.

For instance, going to the gym would be the right thing, while the easy thing would be staying at home. The easy thing would be researching healthy recipes online, and the right thing would be to drive to the store and buy those ingredients. Whatever you do to ease your guilt is never the right thing, and whatever seems most difficult is the most correct course of action.

Unfortunately, doing the right thing usually means doing the hard thing; actually, they are almost always the exact same thing, and that's what this mental model really recognizes. If what you want appears too easy to achieve, you're probably missing something. There are just no shortcuts to the real rewards in life, and you have to engage in a bit of resistance. In a sense, easy things are usually just hard things, only cut short.

People drift toward the path of least resistance in the most unconscious of ways, from doing one fewer exercise at the gym to eating one more bite of ice cream, taking the elevator instead of the stairs, and buying the regular version instead of the diet version of anything. We don't even realize that there are two paths, much less that we are taking the lazy one.

So here's the crux of this mental model: you need to be able to consciously answer whether you are doing *that*—or doing what's *right*. Which path are you on?

When you can't confidently say that you're doing the right thing, *you're not*—and then you are forced to compare the difference between right and easy. If you're not doing what you should be, then anything else out of your mouth is an excuse, plain and simple. Anything that comes after the word "but..." or "it's different because..." or "well..." is the innate recognition that resistance is ahead. That's a good thing.

Instead of beating around the bush and soothing your ego, try stating out loud the two paths you are considering and honestly categorize your actions into right or easy.

You have an hour of free time. Running to lose weight: right thing. Skipping a workout: easy thing. Cutting workout short: easy thing. Driving to buy fast food: easy thing. Committing to a specific portion of food for lunch: right thing. Telling yourself that your foot hurts, so you deserve a break: probably the dishonest yet easy thing.

And when you feel that you are engaging in the easy path of least resistance, ask yourself what the honest reason is. Hint: it's not "it's too hot outside" or "it's too late"; it's actually "I'm not going to run today because I'm lazy and have issues with self-discipline and commitment." In effect, you become brutally honest and confrontational with yourself, which is sometimes the only way to get a message across.

You should always want to answer that you're doing what's right, and that will frequently mean that you have to make a little extra effort. But when you do it consistently, that extra effort pays off. For instance, the magic of compound interest from bank savings accounts. Tiny choices over extended periods of time are what underlie true success and progress.

Doing the right thing may feel like the harder route in the moment, but when you do it consistently, it winds up being the most efficient route to accomplishing your goals.

Inherent in this calculus is the fact that you must actually know what you are aiming towards—what actions are right for what goal? Only when you know the end goal can you say that an action takes you further or closer to it. The end portion of this mental model, how to ensure that you are avoiding the path of least resistance, works best if you have a clear future you can envision. Otherwise, what is all the struggle and resistance for?

So the next time you are battling with yourself between the path of least resistance and the correct path, stop and ask yourself how you will feel 10 minutes, 10 hours, and 10 days from now.

This may not seem so powerful, but it's effective because it forces you to think about your future self and to see how your current path (whichever it is) is going to affect yourself in the future—for better or worse. A lot of times, we may knowingly give in to the temptation of the path of least resistance, but that's not enough to stop us from doing it because we don't have any connection to the consequences. Thinking in terms of 10/10/10 quickly creates that connection.

Why time intervals of 10 minutes, hours, and days? Because that helps you realize how short-term the pleasure/comfort of the path of least resistance is relative to its long-term consequences. At 10 minutes, you might be feeling good, with perhaps just the initial bit of shame creeping in. After 10 hours, you'll feel mostly shame and regret. Ten days later, you'll probably be consumed by regret, having realized some of the negative consequences that your decision or action has had on your pursuit of your long-term goals. You get nothing out of it, and in some cases, you backslide.

For example, imagine that you apply this rule when deciding whether or not to skip a workout to go to dinner with coworkers. If you've just begun exercising and haven't built it into a consistent habit yet, your decision to skip a single workout might increase the odds of skipping future workouts or stopping working out altogether.

How will you feel in 10 minutes, hours, and days? Ten minutes—good, with a slight tinge of regret, as you can still taste the lasagna or ice cream. The pleasure is still tangible. Ten hours—almost entirely regret, as the pleasure is gone and fleeting, and your diet has been soundly broken. Ten days—100% regret, because the broken discipline is now completely meaningless and but a faint memory. The lasagna does not have a lasting benefit, but it does have a lasting cost. Resistance lies between you and what you want.

Takeaways:

- We can't help it; it's how we've been indoctrinated from childhood. Of course, it's not necessarily wrong either. I'm talking about our drive to reach toward achievements instead of avoiding negative consequences. Where other chapters of this book are about mental models, we introduce anti-mental models here to represent how you can achieve just as much if you only focus on one thing: avoidance.
- Mental Model #19: Avoid Direct Goals. Direct goals are like shooting for the moon, while anti-goals, or inverse goals, are about avoiding crashing into the earth and doing everything to prevent that from happening. This has just as good a chance of achieving the outcome you want through direct goals, but it might get you there quicker and more efficiently. Simply articulate the factors involved in a worst-case scenario, then devote your time to preventing them.

- Mental Model #20: Avoiding Thinking Like an Expert. Experts think about the big picture and sometimes can't be bothered with small details. Small details, counterintuitively, are mostly paid attention to by novices, because they are absorbing new information and going slowly through a process. Thinking like an expert in a given field will probably mean that you make small mistakes because you engage in assumptive thinking and focus on overall effects and conception.
- Mental Model #21: Avoid Your Non-Genius Zones. All of us have natural advantages in some things, and despite how hard we work, we will never be more than mediocre in other areas. Recognize your strengths, and while you shouldn't stop trying to improve upon your weaknesses, understand where you will have the most impact.
- Mental Model #22: Avoid To-Do Lists. In fact, construct don't-do lists. Narrowing down what you should be avoiding, and what really doesn't matter, will drastically free up your time. This means

you will have less stress and anxiety and know exactly what your priorities are.

- Mental Model #23: Avoid the Path of Least Resistance. Does something appear too easy? It's too good to be true. Avoid it. Seek resistance, because that's a sign that you are on the right path. On a daily basis, we are faced with two choices: the easy thing and the right thing. We usually don't even realize we have a choice, but when you start to honestly categorize your choices, you might discover that your instinct to avoid resistance is self-sabotage.

Chapter 5. Oldies but Goodies: They're Still Around for a Reason!

At this point of the book, you probably have a good idea of how to use mental models. They are filters for you to strap on in different circumstances to ensure that you are accounting for everything and making the best-informed decision possible. They either help you in domains or scenarios that you are unfamiliar with or can improve with.

The mental models in this last chapter don't necessarily belong to either of those categories. They are all known as *eponymous laws*, which is a fancy term that simply means they were named after someone—usually the person who made the observation or discovery.

That's also where these models differ—they come more from observations of patterns found in real-life, both small and significant. But within them are lessons that can transfer to how you live your life. Some of them might sound familiar, but let's see if the actual definitions and implications differ from the instances you have heard them being used in.

MM #24: Murphy's Law

Use to make sure matters are not left to chance.

Sometimes, we trip on our way to work on the one day that we are wearing white pants. After we arrive to work, we sit in a dirty chair, and now both sides of the white pants are dirty. After work, a basketball bounces into you from the side; now the pants are just filthy from all angles.

Do you ever feel like everything is going wrong and grievance after grievance just piles up like a cascading waterfall? It can be almost like a movie as to how much suffering can suddenly occur. Welcome to the feeling of *Murphy's Law: anything that can go wrong will go wrong*.

If you drop a piece of buttered toast, it will inevitably fall on the buttered side. If you wear white pants, you will inevitably get splashed by a dark liquid. If you just washed your car, a bird will relieve itself on top of the hood. If you just went on a diet, your significant other will somehow bring home a cheesecake they scored for free. You get the idea—if it exists, you will find yourself in the worst possible scenario for whatever you are focusing on.

Most of the time, it is spoken in jest to curse coincidence, and there are some permutations that convey the same feeling of *misfortune at every possible turn*. These include the following:

- Murphy's First Corollary: Left to themselves, things tend to go from bad to   worse.

Any attempt on your part to correct this will only accelerate the process.

- Murphy's Second Corollary: It is impossible to make anything foolproof because fools are so ingenious.

- Murphy's Constant: Matter will be damaged in direct proportion to its value.

- Quantized Revision of Murphy's Law: Everything goes wrong all at once.

- Etorre's Observation: The other line always moves faster.

You probably get the idea by now. Whatever slight possibility there is for something to go poorly *will* be realized. But as you will read later on, there are very practical uses for Murphy's Law.

Murphy's Law is a relatively new concept. In 1928, a magician named Adam Shirk wrote that in a magic act, nine out of ten things that can go wrong usually will. It came to the public consciousness a couple of decades later in 1949, courtesy of an engineer in the United States Air Force named Captain Edward Murphy.

He was consumed by designing airplanes, and as you might guess, things did not go well as a general matter. Through a long series of failed tests and designs, he ended up proclaiming, "If there are two ways to do something, and one of those ways will result in disaster, he'll do it that way." This eventually found its way too its current form of "anything that can go wrong will go wrong," and subsequently it became a kind of warning among Air Force engineers and designers.

Eventually, it came to light that the Air Force's near-spotless safety record was due to its belief in Murphy's Law and how it would encounter double-checking, confirmation, and rigorous testing of fail-safes and redundancies.

And that's where the mental model portion of Murphy's Law comes in. It reminds us that just about everything is subject to failure and error. Sometimes a failure represents a coincidence that simply could not be prevented or predicted. Other times, a failure represents a systematic series of errors in which failure was inevitable.

For instance, how would Murphy's Law influence a skydiver? A parachute is a pretty good idea for a skydiver. Having an extra parachute is an even better idea. And having the third is equally as bright.

Murphy's Law is behind the fail-safes, backup plans, and contingency plans of our world. It reminds us to double-check, even when we're 99% sure about something. What percentage of the time does a skydiver's parachute malfunction? It's probably infinitesimal, but I'm betting you wouldn't jump out of an airplane using a parachute that hasn't been recently checked.

Relying on humans is not a smart move because humans are, by and large, careless idiots—myself absolutely included.

If you think everything has gone to plan, it probably hasn't. This can apply to almost any human endeavor—from a child taking a math test to an electrician repairing an oven, a chef cooking a lobster, and a rocket scientist blasting a spaceship into outer space. If you keep Murphy's Law in mind, you can drastically change the way with which you approach certainty.

What *are* the small cracks in which Murphy's Law could take hold? What truly needs verification/confirmation? What part of my plan (recipe, test, task) am I quietly hoping will be *good enough to get by*? Plan for the worst-case scenario, and much like anti-mental models, seek to avoid what you *don't* want, as opposed to aiming toward what you *do* want.

You might get away with it, but that's not a mindset you should be relying upon.

MM #25: Occam's Razor

Use to determine the likelihood of anything.

If you claim to see a "flying entity" in the sky, what do you believe it would be?

A. The spaceship of the lizard people, coming to take back their planet.

B. Ancient remnants of whoever built the pyramids. Maybe the lizard people?

C. The resurrection of Zeus, king of the ancient Greek gods of Olympus.

D. None of the above.

Now, there are many compelling reasons for you to choose D. But Occam's Razor articulates the strongest reason: the simpler, the higher the likelihood of truth.

When seeking explanations for events or situations, you might try to analyze it with a variety of approaches and theories—each more complex than the previous. These are options A, B, and C.

While this kind of brainstorming can pay dividends, it's not always the best course of action for one simple reason: the more factors you have, the less probability there is of it being correct. Thus, the fewer factors involved, the higher the probability of it being correct.

That's the heart of the Occam's Razor principle, which was championed by 14th-century theologian and philosopher William of Ockham (the spelling has changed over time).

Occam's Razor was originally expressed as "Entities should not be multiplied beyond necessity"—simply, one should not over-complicate problem-solving by bringing in too many extra hypotheses, variables, or extraneous factors. Drawing from that original principle, Occam's Razor is often stated in present times as "*The simplest explanation is usually the correct one*" as well as "The more assumptions you have to make, the more unlikely that explanation is."

That's why answer D is correct. It's the simplest answer with the fewest variables involved. Thus, it is the most likely explanation.

Your initial instinct, oddly enough, is not to go with the simplest answer with the fewest variables. We usually go with the most *available*, *accessible*, or *alarming* explanation, which tends to represent what we either want to see in a situation or absolutely *don't* want to see.

For instance, you wake up one clear summer morning to find that your outside trash can was overturned during the night, and your garbage is all over the driveway. You could develop several different theories as to how that happened:

- A bolt of lightning came down from the skies, zapped your garbage can, and knocked it over.

- A youth gang bent on causing disruption and mayhem decided to attack your garbage can.

- An extraterrestrial spider slipped through a wormhole in the cosmos and went through your garbage can looking for a substance that would lead it back to its home planet.

- One of the neighborhood raccoons knocked your garbage can over while looking for food.

According to Occam's Razor, the correct answer is probably the simplest—the one that doesn't require a bunch of unrealistic theories or mental detours to explain. The fewer the variables, the better—the raccoon is only one, and a variable that at least has some chance of being real.

With the other three possibilities, you'd have to make some rather complicated explanations as to how they could happen. Each additional factor you add in substantially decreases the overall probability.

How could there be lightning on a clear summer night? Is it really likely that a gang would get their kicks by messing with people's garbage cans? Are extraterrestrial spiders really that incompetent to need something from your garbage?

This particular example is a bit over the top, but the Occam's Razor principle can be employed in everyday situations when we're trying to decipher or explain the issues around a certain event. The more complicated or labyrinthine the explanations get, the less likely they are to be the truth. Life is not the plot to the movie *Inception*.

This mental model encourages us to *start* with the simplest explanation and add in additional factors carefully and slowly, one at a time. Occam's Razor is a *principle*, not a rule. Sometimes the simplest answer *won't* in fact be the truth; it may well be something that has a lot of complex factors. Not *every* complicated scenario should be discounted. Furthermore, if the simple answer doesn't take hard evidence or data into account, then it's still invalid—it shouldn't be something that's easy to understand but not backed up by provable means.

But Occam's Razor is almost always the best way to *begin to approach* a problem. Consider the most easily explained, simple, and realistic interpretation of a certain event, and only contemplate more intricate explanations if they seem reasonable.

Excessive elaboration or unnecessary elements will only distract you from the original problem. Don't let your creative instincts play too much of a part when trying to understand a situation—more often than not, the most elementary, basic solution is the most accurate.

MM #26: Hanlon's Razor

Use to explain actions by giving others the benefit of the doubt.

Though the world is complex, it often works out in simplistic and direct ways. That's what Occam's Razor encourages, and Hanlon's Razor does the same in a slightly different way.

It was originated in 1774 by Robert Hanlon as *"Never attribute to malice that which can be adequately explained by neglect."* The most modern and widespread version is *"Never ascribe to malice that which is adequately explained by incompetence"* and is often attributed to Napoleon Bonaparte, though author Robert Heinlein has a strong claim to it.

So how does this relate to Occam's Razor and the preference for simple explanations with as few variables as possible? Because making assumptions about someone's intentions and motivations based on their actions is, well, a rather large assumption. The most likely cause for malice, or any other negative intention, is neglect or incompetence.

In other words, it's easier for a person to do something negative out of neglect or incompetence, and it takes another few steps to truly be able to say that malice is the cause. Being that we are not a species with psychic powers, we will never know people's intentions.

This mental model assumes simplicity in the realm of social interaction. If you presume that people only want to be good to you, it has the power to massively improve your relationships.

Suppose that you want a particular brand of cereal at the grocery store, yet someone two feet in front of you grabs the last box.

You are feeling cheeky and angry enough to confront them about it, and so you exclaim, "Do you know how much I wanted that? You're so inconsiderate!" They never even turn around. Later, you discover while watching them in the checkout lane that they are actually deaf and didn't hear your words.

Cue feeling like a fool. You've just created anxiety and rage in a situation where it didn't need to exist. You could have kept your cool and let things roll off your back, but you didn't. Hanlon's Razor forces you to take your offended ego out of a situation and analyze it with everyone's best intentions in mind. People are oblivious and thoughtless at times, including you, but it usually doesn't mean what you think it means. Empathy is a mental model in itself.

And yet, this doesn't mean we should lower our guards. When you apply this mental model to everything and everyone, you gain a type of blindness to malice. That's dangerous—the person walking behind you late at night, following you after five turns, is likely not doing so out of neglect or incompetence.

MM #27: The Pareto Principle

Use to find where your time and resources will create the biggest impact.

I can distinctly remember when I first began writing more and more. I spent a lot of time spinning my wheels on things that ultimately didn't matter, though I didn't know it at the time. This can easily spiral into perfectionism and analysis paralysis, and I was no exception.

Because I felt incredibly invested and wanted to impart as much value as possible, I spent an inordinate amount of time on small changes and edits that no one besides me would ever notice. I suppose my heart was in the right place, but that's not what makes a business succeed.

The overall message and effectiveness were largely the same, but I would rework sentences over and over until I was satisfied with them. Consequently, it took almost a year to write and edit my first book. This isn't to say that quality control isn't important. However, I now realize there's no sense in agonizing over every word choice in a book, especially if the overall message and effectiveness will not change or be improved. What matters in a book, anyway? In fiction, the plot and characters. In non-fiction, clear lessons. In any case, not what I was spending all of my time on. In any pursuit, only a few things really make the difference, and tinkering with the tiny things is usually a worthless pursuit.

The primary reason for this is the *80/20 rule*, otherwise known as *the Pareto Principle*, our eponymous law turned mental model.

The Pareto Principle was named for an Italian economist who accurately noted that 80% of the real estate in Italy was owned by only 20% of the population. He began to wonder if the same kind of distribution applied to other aspects of life. In fact, he was correct.

The Pareto Principle applies to everything about the human experience: our work, relationships, career, grades, hobbies, and interests. Most things follow a Pareto distribution, where there is a fairly skewed ratio between input and output. It's about finding the best bang for your buck.

- 80% of the results you want out of a task will be produced by 20% of your activities and efforts directed toward it.
- 20% of the tasks go toward creating 80% of the profit.
- 80% of the happiness you get will be from 20% of the pictures.
- 20% of tasks will make a difference to 80% of a project's success.
- 80% of your problems in life are caused by 20% of the same people.
- 20% of your wardrobe gets 80% of the wear.

In a way, this is related to a mental model from an earlier chapter on diminishing returns. The more you spend above 20% on something, the more your returns will diminish. Thus, unless you have an extremely clear goal to bring something to optimal performance or efficiency, you should just focus on that specific 20% rather than the other 80% of tasks.

This mental model has one simple proposition and lesson: identify the 20% input that generates the 80% output in an area you are seeking to improve and focus on that. Don't try to do everything at once; just focus on what actually moves the needle and creates more of the result you want.

For instance, if you set a goal of trying to lose weight, you will lose 80% of the weight by just doing 20% of the actions you think you should, such as drinking more water to combat feelings of hunger and hitting the gym three times a week. Everything else, like counting every calorie, lugging around Tupperware filled with broccoli and chicken, going on crash diets, sweating off weight in saunas—that's the 80% effort that will only create 20% of the results. Therefore, focus on doing those 20%

actions as best you can, and ignore the rest. Engaging in those 80% actions is fairly useless unless you want to become a fitness model.

If your business sells a range of products but 80% of the sales comes from a small subset of Mickey Mouse-themed products, what do you think you should do? Probably drop the other products and expand on the Mickey Mouse products.

Tasks that you think make a difference actually don't—not to your bottom line, not to your end result, and not to the people you fear judgment from. Those tasks amount to trivialities, similar to what we'll cover soon in MM #30. The aim is not to cut corners, but rather to maximizing efficiency.

The application is quite clear in work and productivity contexts. When it comes to general life enjoyment through activities or relationships, it works the same; you just have to replace "how to make **more** money with **less** work" with "how to be **happier** with *less* work." The same issues all transfer; 20% of your relationships will create 80% of your happiness, and 80% of your enjoyment is caused by 20% of your hobbies.

The Pareto Principle is a mental model that encourages efficiency and the greatest ratio of input to output. What are the tasks that make the biggest impact, regardless of details or completion? Do those first and foremost—they might adequate for your purposes. Become results-driven and don't get caught up in what doesn't matter.

MM #28: Sturgeon's Law

Use to be more discerning and protective of your mental resources.

Originally called "Sturgeon's Revelation," this guideline was first brought to mind by science fiction writer Theodore Sturgeon (1918–1985).

In a 1958 column, he found himself defending his chosen genre, since science fiction of the time hadn't quite begun to transcend its reputation as mere pulp fiction. Sturgeon felt that critics were basing their opinions of science fiction on its worst examples. "Using the same standards that 90% of science fiction is trash, crud, or crap, it can be argued that 90% of film, literature, consumer goods, etc. is crap."

And thus, Sturgeon's Law was born: *"90% of everything is crap."*

The maxim took on a life of its own after Sturgeon used it to describe art and products. It came to mean that since the heavy preponderance of what we consume, read, watch, or review is crap, we need to spend much less time obsessing or even regarding it. Instead, we should focus on the 10% that's meaningful and enlightening or otherwise beneficial to us in some way.

Sturgeon's Law is basically a more colorful, more restrictive version of the Pareto Principle. And just like the Pareto Principle, it can be applied to just about every aspect of life. Sturgeon's Law just sets an even higher standard for us to aspire to.

For the purposes of our discussion, Sturgeon's Law means that the vast majority of information is low-quality. You could even say that 90% of what we *think* about on a daily basis isn't worth the time. And that's true to an extent. Our brains make a million neural connections every day—certainly most of them aren't necessary or even useful.

With clear thinking, Sturgeon's Law works in a twofold way. First, consider that much of the information we might use to assess something is inessential, poorly constructed, insignificant, or just plain wrong. Second, we shouldn't get too consumed by how terrible these parts are; rather, we should focus on the thinking and processes that are good.

When we're trying to solve a problem or understand something, therefore, we should concentrate on the most vital components or the most reliable, provable information. Don't waste a lot of energy on the most common flaws or the most disparaged elements. Sturgeon's Law says its low quality makes it unimportant, so it's dispensable. And as Occam's Razor suggests, giving too much attention to the inessential will only knock essential thinking off-course.

There are a couple of caveats to Sturgeon's Law, of course. Everyone's standards are relative, and some things we personally consider to be crap will be someone else's gold. The ratio can vary, too: in certain cases, you may only have 75% crap. And within that 10% of non-crap, not all of it will be absolutely great. Some of it is only slightly better than crap.

But as a way to clarify and streamline one's thinking, and to counteract some of our mind's tendency to wander in petty or irrelevant directions, Sturgeon's Law is definitely a non-crappy approach you can take. Find the definitively non-crap 10% and work your way out from there. In the end, this mental model preaches selectivity with your time and energy and being perpetually skeptical about what you allow into your life.

MM #29-30: Parkinson's Laws

Use to stop procrastinating and get more done in less time.

British historian Cyril Parkinson was a man of many talents, but for the purposes of this mental model, we'll focus on the two eponymous laws that were eventually named after him, both of which were related to productivity.

The first of these laws is called *Parkinson's Law of Triviality,* also known as the bike shed effect. The story behind the law is that there was a committee tasked with designing a nuclear power plant. This was obviously a large undertaking, so appropriate care had to be taken in addressing the safety mechanisms and environmental implications of building a new nuclear power plant.

The committee met regularly and was able to quell most safety and environmental concerns. They were even able to ensure the nuclear power plant had a pleasing aesthetic that would surely attract the best engineers.

However, as the committee met to deal with the remaining issues, one issue in particular kept popping up: the design of the bike shed for employees that commuted by bicycle.

This included the color, the signage, the materials used, and the type of bike rack to be installed. The committee couldn't get past these details—details that were meaningless in the greater scope of a functioning nuclear power plant. They kept fixating on small, trivial features that were a matter of opinion and subjectivity.

Parkinson summarized the bike shed fiasco in the following manner: "The time spent on any item of the agenda will be in inverse proportion to the sum [of money] involved."

Therein lies the essence of Parkinson's Law of Triviality. People are prone to overthinking and fixating on small details that don't matter in the grand scheme of a task, and they do so to the detriment of larger issues that have infinitely more importance. People unwittingly give a disproportionate amount of time and attention to trivialities; these are the tasks that, if you were to take a step back and evaluate, would compel you to ask, *"Who the heck cares about this?"*

This is the classic case of not being able to see the forest for the trees (remind you of another mental model from earlier in the book?) and unwittingly keeping yourself from the finish line. There are two main reasons for this phenomenon.

The first reason is procrastination and avoidance. When people want to procrastinate on an issue, they often try to remain productive by doing something that is perceived as productive. Trivial details are still details that need to be taken care of at some point, and they are things that we can tweak endlessly. We feel that we are doing something instead of imitating living the life of a couch potato.

This is why we clean when we are putting off work. We're subconsciously avoiding the work but making ourselves feel better by thinking, "*At least something productive got done!*"

Fixating on the trivial is the equivalent of cleaning the bathroom to avoid work. You are being productive in some way, but not in a way that aids your overall goal. That's why when the committee members were stuck on how to tackle all of the safety issues, they defaulted to something they *could* theoretically solve: a bike shed.

Trivial tasks need to be addressed at some point, but you need to evaluate when you should actually address them. Triviality can easily sneak into our lives as a placebo for real productivity.

Second, and this refers more to group situations, the Law of Triviality may be the result of individuals who wish to contribute in any way they can but find themselves unable to in all but the most trivial of matters. They're on the committee, but they don't have the knowledge or expertise to contribute to more significant issues.

Yet everyone can visualize a cheap, simple bicycle shed, so planning one can result in endless discussions, because everyone involved wants to add a touch, show contribution, and demonstrate their intelligence. It's completely self-serving.

The main and only reason to call meetings is to solve big problems that require input from multiple people. Locking people in a room and letting them brainstorm is a fairly proven method for getting things done—*if* you have an agenda that you stick to. Anything else should be addressed independently; otherwise, the level of discussion inevitably falls to the lowest common denominator in the room.

If somebody starts talking about something that's not on the agenda, you know that triviality is on your doorstep. If somebody is spinning their wheels regarding a tiny aspect of a larger project, triviality is already in the room. If you find yourself suddenly compelled to organize your sock drawer while working on a particularly tough issue, triviality has made a cup of tea and is making itself comfortable.

When you devolve into small tasks that may not need tweaking or do not impact your overall goal, it's time to take a break and recharge instead of pretending to be productive.

The key to utilizing this mental model and combatting triviality is threefold: (1) have a strict agenda, whether it is your to-do list or calendar or other technique, so you know what you should focus on and what you should ignore; (2) know your overall goals for the day and constantly ask yourself if what you're doing is contributing to them or avoiding them; and (3) develop an awareness of when you're starting to lose energy so you can preempt triviality from occurring.

Knowing is half the battle when it comes to beating Parkinson's Law of Triviality.

Parkinson's other law is simply known as *Parkinson's Law*, and it is arguably more well-known. One of the things that people who procrastinate a lot might say to justify it is that they work better under a time crunch: "I work best with a deadline!"

Parkinson's Law states that *work expands so as to fill the time available for its completion.* Whatever deadline you give yourself, big or small, that's how long you'll take to complete the work. If you give yourself a relaxed deadline, you avoid being disciplined; if you give yourself a tight deadline, you can draw on your self-discipline.

Parkinson observed that as bureaucracies expanded, their efficiency decreased instead of increased. The more space and time people were given, the more they took—something that he realized was applicable to a wide range of other circumstances. The general form of the law became that increasing the size of something decreases its efficiency.

As it relates to focus and time, Parkinson found that simple tasks would be made increasingly more complex in order to fill the time allotted to their completion. Decreasing the available time for completing a task caused that task to become simpler and easier and completed in a timelier fashion.

Building on Parkinson's Law, a study of college students found that those who imposed strict deadlines on themselves for completing assignments consistently performed better than those who gave themselves an excessive amount of time and those who set no limits at all. Why?

The artificial limitations they had set for their work caused them to be far more efficient than their counterparts. They didn't spend a lot of time worrying about the assignments because they didn't give themselves the time to indulge. They got to work, finished the projects, and moved on. They also didn't have time to ruminate on what ultimately didn't matter—a very common type of subtle procrastination.

They were able to subconsciously focus on only the elements that mattered in completing the assignment.

Very few people are ever going to require you or even ask you to work less. So if you want to be more productive and efficient, you'll have to avoid falling victim to Parkinson's Law yourself by applying artificial limitations on the time you give yourself to complete tasks. By simply giving yourself time limits and deadlines for your work, you force yourself to focus on the crucial elements of the task. You don't make things more complex or difficult than they need to be just to fill the time.

For example, say that your supervisor gives you a spreadsheet and asks you to make a few charts from it by the end of the week. The task might take an hour, but after looking over the spreadsheet you notice that it's disorganized and difficult to read, so you start editing it. This takes an entire week, but the charts you were supposed to generate would only have taken an hour. If you had been given the deadline of one day, you would have simply focused on the charts and ignored everything that wasn't important. When we are given the space, as Parkinson's Law dictates, we expand our work to fill the time.

Set aggressive deadlines so that you are actually challenging yourself on a consistent basis, and you'll avoid this pitfall. A distant deadline also typically means a sustained level of background stress—push yourself to finish early and free your mind. Save your time by giving yourself less time.

Takeaways:

- Mental Model #24: Murphy's Law: Anything that can go wrong will go wrong, so make sure it doesn't have the opportunity. Don't rely on just getting by; make sure that you are as fail-safe as possible.
- Mental Model #25: Occam's Razor: The simplest explanation with the fewest variables is most likely to be the correct one. Our instinct is to go for the most mentally available explanation, which

says more about what we want to see or avoid.

- Mental Model #26: Hanlon's Razor: Malicious acts are far more likely to be explained by incompetence, stupidity, or neglect; assumptions about one's intentions are likely to be wrong. Improve your relationships by giving the benefit of the doubt and assuming, at worst, absent-mindedness.
- Mental Model #27: Pareto Principle: There is a natural distribution that tends to occur, where 20% of the actions we take are responsible for 80% of the results; thus, we should focus on the 20% for maximum input-to-output ratio. This is in the name of becoming results-driven and simply following what the data is telling you. This is not about cutting corners; it is about understanding what causes an impact.
- Mental Model #28: Sturgeon's Law: 90% of everything is crap, so be selective with your time and energy. Start with the 10% absolute non-crap and slowly work your way out. This is a more

restrictive version of the Pareto Principle in some ways.

- Mental Model #29-30: Parkinson's Laws: First, triviality can easily set in because it feels good to feel productive (even in minute ways) and voice your opinion. Know your real priorities and ask if progress is actually being made toward them. Second, work expands to fill the time it is given, so give it less time. Wanting to work at a relaxed pace often just causes self-sabotage.

Summary Guide

Chapter 1. Decision-Making for Speed and Context

- Mental models are blueprints we can use in various contexts to make sense of the world, interpret information correctly, and understand our context. They give us predictable outcomes. A recipe is the most basic form of mental model; each ingredient has its role, time, and place. However, a recipe is not applicable to anything outside the realm of food. Thus, we find ourselves in a position of wanting to learn a wide range of mental models (or latticework, as Charlie Munger puts it) to prepare ourselves for whatever may come our way. We can't learn ones for each individual scenario, but we *can* find widely applicable ones. In this chapter, we start with mental models for smarter and quicker decision-making.

- Mental Model #1: Address "Important"; Ignore "Urgent." These are entirely separate things that we often fuse together. Important is what truly matters, even if the payoff or deadline is not so immediate. Urgent only refers to the speed of response that is desired. You can easily use an Eisenhower Matrix to clarify your priorities and ignore urgent tasks, unless they so happen to also be important.

- Mental Model #2: Visualize All the Dominoes. We are a shortsighted species. We think only one step ahead in terms of consequences, and then we typically only limit it to our own consequences. We need to engage in second-order thinking and visualize all the dominos that could be falling. Without this, it can't be said that you are making a well-informed decision.

- Mental Model #3: Make Reversible Decisions. Most of them are; some of them aren't. But we aren't doing ourselves any favors when we assume that they are all irreversible, because it keeps us in indecision far too long. Create an action bias for reversible decisions, as there is nothing to lose and only information and speed to gain.

- Mental Model #4: Seek "Satisfiction." This is a mixture of satisfy and suffice, and it is aiming to make decisions that are good enough, adequate, and serve their purpose. This stands in stark contrast to those who wish to maximize their decisions with "just in case" and "that sounds nice" extras. Those who maximize are looking to make a perfect choice. This doesn't exist, so they are usually just left waiting.

- Mental Model #5: Stay Within 40–70%. This is Colin Powell's rule. Make a decision with no less than 40% of the information you need but no more than 70%. Anything less and you are just guessing; anything more and you are just wasting time. You can replace "information" with just about anything, and you will realize that this mental model is about encouraging quick yet informed decisions.

- Mental Model #6: Minimize Regret. Jeff Bezos developed what he calls the regret minimization framework. In it, he asks one to visualize themselves at age 80 and ask if they would regret making (or not making) a decision. This simplifies decisions by making them about one metric: regret.

Chapter 2. How to See More Clearly

- Seeing and thinking clearly is not something we instinctually do. Humans are all about survival, pleasure, avoiding pain, food, sex, and sleep. Everything else that we would consider a higher pursuit tends to come second, at least in our brains. Thus, mental models to ensure that we are thinking clearly are of the utmost importance. The world usually looks different at second glance.

- Mental Model #7: Ignore "Black Swans." This is the first mental model that specifically warns against our tendency to jump to conclusions based on imperfect, skewed, or incomplete information. A black swan event is an entirely unpredictable event that comes out of nowhere. In doing so, it skews all data and beliefs, and people start to take the black swan into account as a new normal. But these are just outliers that should be ignored.

- Mental Model #8: Look for Equilibrium Points. This mental model is about noticing trends in progress. When you first start something, you go from zero to one—that's an infinite rate of progress. Then you go from one to two, two to three, and so on, and the rate of progress slows, and the returns start diminishing. Somewhere around there is an equilibrium point that truly represents what the average mean will be. Don't make the mistake of not waiting for it.

- Mental Model #9: Wait for the Regression to the Mean. This is the final mental model about seeing the whole picture in terms of information. A change without a *reason* for the change is not really a change; it's just a deviation. As such, it doesn't represent what will continue to happen in the future. A regression to the mean is when things settle back down and resume what they were doing before—this is representative of reality.

- Mental Model #10: What Would Bayes Do (WWBD)? Funnily enough, the previous three mental models were about our flawed attempts to draw conclusions and predict the future. Bayes' Theorem is something that actually does allow us to draw conclusions about the future: based on probabilities and taking into account events that have already occurred. All you need are the rough probabilities of three elements to plug into the Bayes' formula, and you will come to a more accurate conclusion than so-called experts. This is basic probabilistic thinking.

- Mental Model #11: Do It Like Darwin. Darwin apparently was not a genius, but he did have one trait that set him apart from others: his undying devotion to truth. In doing, he developed his golden rule (and our mental model) of giving equal weight and attention to arguments and opinions that opposed his own. Instead of growing defensive when presented with something that opposed him, he grew critical and skeptical toward himself. This radical open-mindedness puts aside confirmation bias and ego.

- Mental Model #12: Think With System 2. We each have two systems of thought, courtesy of Daniel Kahneman: System 1 and System 2. System 1 focuses on speed and efficiency of thought, while System 2 focuses on accuracy and depth of thought. System 2 is smart, while System 1 is dumb. System 1 does more harm than good, but unfortunately, it is the one we default to because it is easier. Gain awareness of the difference between the two; acknowledge System 1, then try to jump immediately to System 2.

Chapter 3. Eye-Opening Problem-Solving

- Most of the ways we solve problems amount to running into the same wall and hoping that it will eventually crumble. Obviously, this is not optimal for us or the wall. Better problem-solving can certainly stem from mental models because they can provide a formula for us to follow. After all, that's all things like the quadratic equation or π are—mental models to help us solve problems.

- Mental Model #13: Peer Review Your Perspectives. Many of the ways we fail at solving problems are related to our inability to look at other perspectives. In fact, we should be continually checking our perspectives through triangulation against those of others. Thinking and solving in a vacuum will never work because if you didn't experience it firsthand, it won't make sense to you.

- Mental Model #14: Find Your Own Flaws. This mental model is about resisting the comforting allure of confirmation bias and attempting to scrutinize yourself before others ever get the chance. Assume that you are wrong; this especially applies to interpersonal relationships. If you assume that you are at least 1% responsible for conflict, then your illusion of superiority and infallibility is broken, an important factor in social interaction.

- Mental Model #15: Separate Correlation From Causation. They are entirely different things. Forcing a relationship where none exists will cause you to chase the wrong issue. In addition, you must separate proximate cause from root cause—root cause is what we always want, and it can be reached through a series of questions.

- Mental Model #16 Storytell in Reverse. When it comes to causation, sometimes we just need to get better at thinking in a certain manner. You have a visual aid in a fishbone diagram, which goes on to document causes of causes and so on. This is storytelling in reverse because you start with a conclusion and you work backward through sometimes ambiguous means.

- Mental Model #17: SCAMPER It. The SCAMPER method stands for seven techniques that help direct thinking toward novel ideas and solutions: (S) substitute, (C) combine, (A) adapt, (M) minimize/magnify, (P) put to another use, (E) eliminate, and (R) reverse.

- Mental Model #18: Get Back to First Principles. When we try to solve problems, oftentimes we attempt to follow methods or a specific path just because they are the conventional means. But are they the best? First principles thinking strips away assumptions and leaves you with only a set of facts and a desired outcome. From there, you can forge your own solution.

Chapter 4. Anti-Mental Models: How Avoidance Breeds Success

- We can't help it; it's how we've been indoctrinated from childhood. Of course, it's not necessarily wrong either. I'm talking about our drive to reach toward achievements instead of avoiding negative consequences. Where other chapters of this book are about mental models, we introduce anti-mental models here to represent how you can achieve just as much if you only focus on one thing: avoidance.

- Mental Model #19: Avoid Direct Goals. Direct goals are like shooting for the moon, while anti-goals, or inverse goals, are about avoiding falling and doing everything to prevent that from happening. This has just as good a chance of achieving the outcome you want through direct goals, but it might get you there quicker and more efficiently. Simply articulate the factors involved in a worst-case scenario, then devote your time to preventing them.

- Mental Model #20: Avoiding Thinking Like an Expert. Experts think about the big picture and sometimes can't be bothered with small details. Small details, counterintuitively, are mostly paid attention to by novices, because they are absorbing new information and going slowly through a process. Thinking like an expert in a given field will probably mean that you make small mistakes because you engage in assumptive thinking and focus on overall effects and conception.

- Mental Model #21: Avoid Your Non-Genius Zones. All of us have natural advantages in some things, and despite how hard we work, we will never be more than mediocre in other areas. Recognize your strengths, and while you shouldn't stop trying to improve upon your weaknesses, understand where you will have the most impact.

- Mental Model #22: Avoid To-Do Lists. In fact, construct don't-do lists. Narrowing down what you should be avoiding, and what really doesn't matter, will drastically free up your time. This means you will have less stress and anxiety and know exactly what your priorities are.

- Mental Model #23: Avoid the Path of Least Resistance. Does something appear too easy? It's too good to be true. Avoid it. Seek resistance, because that's a sign that you are on the right path. On a daily basis, we are faced with two choices: the easy thing and the right thing. We usually don't even realize we have a choice, but when you start to honestly categorize your choices, you might realize that behavior change is needed.

Chapter 5. Oldies but Goodies: They're Still Around for a Reason!

- Mental Model #24: Murphy's Law: Anything that can go wrong will go wrong, so make sure it doesn't have the opportunity. Don't rely on just getting by; make sure that you are as fail-safe as possible.
- Mental Model #25: Occam's Razor: The simplest explanation with the fewest variables is most likely to be the correct one. Our instinct is to go for the most mentally available explanation, which says more about what we want to see or avoid.
- Mental Model #26: Hanlon's Razor: Malicious acts are far more likely to be

explained by incompetence, stupidity, or neglect; assumptions about one's intentions are likely to be wrong. Improve your relationships by giving the benefit of the doubt and assuming, at worst, absent-mindedness.

- Mental Model #27: Pareto Principle: There is a natural distribution that tends to occur, where 20% of the actions we take are responsible for 80% of the results; thus, we should focus on the 20% for maximum input-to-output ratio. This is in the name of becoming results-driven and simply following what the data is telling you. This is not about cutting corners; it is about understanding what causes an impact.

- Mental Model #28: Sturgeon's Law: Ninety percent of everything is crap, so be selective with your time. Start with the 10% absolute non-crap and slowly work your way out.

- Mental Model #29-30: Parkinson's Laws: First, triviality can easily set in because it feels good to feel productive and voice your opinion. Know your real priorities and ask if progress is actually being made toward them. Second, work expands to fill the time it is given, so give it less time. Wanting to work at a relaxed pace often just causes self-sabotage.

Printed in the USA
CPSIA information can be obtained
at www.ICGtesting.com
LVHW011644271223
767218LV00007B/261